T0301977

ISSUES IN
GOVERNANCE,
GROWTH AND
GLOBALIZATION
IN
ASIA

ISSUES IN
GOVERNANCE,
GROWTH AND
GLOBALIZATION
IN ASIA

Editors

Tony Cavoli
University of South Australia, Australia

Siona Listokin
George Mason University, USA

Ramkishen S Rajan
George Mason University, USA

World Scientific

NEW JERSEY • LONDON • SINGAPORE • BEIJING • SHANGHAI • HONG KONG • TAIPEI • CHENNAI

Published by

World Scientific Publishing Co. Pte. Ltd.

5 Toh Tuck Link, Singapore 596224

USA office: 27 Warren Street, Suite 401-402, Hackensack, NJ 07601

UK office: 57 Shelton Street, Covent Garden, London WC2H 9HE

Library of Congress Cataloging-in-Publication Data
Issues in governance, growth and globalization in Asia / editors, Tony Cavoli, University of South Australia, Australia, Siona Listokin, George Mason University, USA, Ramkishen S. Rajan, George Mason University.
    pages cm
  Includes bibliographical references and index.
  ISBN 978-9814504942 (alk. paper)
  1. Asia--Economic conditions--21st century. 2. Asia--Economic policy. 3. Economic development--Asia. 4. Corporate governance--Asia. 5. Globalization--Economic aspects--Asia. I. Cavoli, Tony, editor of compilation. II. Listokin, Siona, editor of compilation. III. Rajan, Ramkishen S., editor of compilation. IV. Chen, En-Te. Convergence in the ownership and governance of East Asian firms.
  HC412.I787 2014
  330.95--dc23

                                        2014000205

British Library Cataloguing-in-Publication Data
A catalogue record for this book is available from the British Library.

In-house Editor: DONG Lixi

Typeset by Stallion Press
Email: enquiries@stallionpress.com

Printed in Singapore

Contents

Contributors

Tony Cavoli
School of Commerce, University of South Australia

En-Te Chen
School of Economics and Finance
Queensland University of Technology

Stephen Gray
UQ Business School, University of Queensland

Rabin Hattari
Asian Development Bank

Andrew Hughes-Hallett
School of Public Policy, George Mason University

Jan Libich
School of Economics and Finance, LaTrobe University
Centre for Applied Macroeconomic Analysis

Siona Listokin
School of Public Policy, George Mason University

Sonia Ketkar
School of Public Policy and Center for Emerging Markets Policies,
George Mason University

Ron McIver
School of Commerce, University of South Australia

John Nowland
Department of Accountancy, City University of Hong Kong

Ramkishen S. Rajan
School of Public Policy, George Mason University

Petr Stehlik
University of West Bohemia

Shandre Thangavelu
Department of Economics, National University of Singapore

Chapter 1

Introduction and Overview

Tony Cavoli, Siona Listokin and Ramkishen S Rajan

1.1 Introduction

Asian countries have the dubious distinction of being both the major actors and reluctant participants in the two major economic crises of the past quarter century. Both the Asian and Global Financial Crises of 1997–1998 and 2007–2009, respectively, initiated significant changes in the financial, governance and political-economy structures of the region, though frequently in dissimilar ways. Following the Asian crisis, policymakers and academics issued cries for institutional reform at the state and firm levels; in many cases, reform was actually implemented rather than simply rhetorical. The region's recent history of shock and reform has implications for the rest of the world today. In retrospect, the experiences of Asian countries in the decade between the two crises offer critical case studies of economic decline and recovery, policy development and governance changes.

Trade in the region offers an immediate example: following the Asian crisis the trajectory of regional economic growth in Southeast Asia diverged, as some countries increased their trade dependence and the group of relevant local partners expanded to include other parts of East and Central Asia. These shifts had implications (many of which are still becoming clear) as the global financial crisis reverberated throughout the world. Asia as a whole experienced a relatively small retraction while individual countries within the region dealt with the unfortunate consequences of economic integration in a deep global recession.

While much of the literature following the Asian crisis emphasized regional economic growth and the development state, the recent crisis highlights the need to focus on the system of global networks that simultaneously strengthens the region and leaves it vulnerable to external shocks. Indeed, in contrast to the Asian crisis, the very nature of the Global Financial Crisis (GFC) was external, with developments that impacted countries through global connections of investment, corporate governance and macroeconomic policy. The role of the development or regulatory state in the context of external shocks is less important than it had been in 1997–1998, and it is not unreasonable to predict that the scholarly and policy lessons from the recent crisis will focus considerably less on internal reform, rather than re-examining the interaction of global networks and domestic policy.

The Association of Southeast Asian Nations (ASEAN) leaders said as much in March 2009, following a meeting to discuss the global economic and financial crisis:

> "... [W]hile ASEAN's economic fundamentals remain sound as a result of significant structural reforms undertaken since the 1997/98 Asian financial crisis, the deepening global economic downturn, coupled with heightened risk aversion in financial markets, have adversely impacted trade and investment in the region."[1]

The communiqué followed to emphasize the need for coordinated global reform of the international financial system.

Global networks of investment, corporate governance and macro policy thus require additional examination. While the general level of integration within Asia and beyond has grown, there is considerable country-level variation that sheds light on economic opportunity and vulnerability. At the macro level, the global networks have greatly influenced exchange rate and stability policy. At the micro level, global networks have created institutional shifts in governance at the industry and firm levels.

This volume addresses these and other themes related to the current state and future development of Asia and beyond. The work is the product of a research workshop at the Institute of Southeast Asian Studies (ISEAS) held in Singapore in October 2010. The first section addresses corporate governance within firms located in Asia and as entities participating in corporate ownership elsewhere. Next, the key issues of globalization are directly

---

[1]Available at http://www.asean.org/asean/asean-summit/item/press-statement-on-the-global-economic-and-financial-crisis.

addressed, including foreign direct investment (FDI) into the region, integration among Southeast Asian countries with the rest of Asia, and multinational enterprise investment strategy in Asia following initial entry decisions. In the final section, the macroeconomic policies of state actors, and the effects of economic growth are examined. These chapters include theoretical models and empirical work on central bank independence, inflation targets and currency markets.

This book will be of importance to a range of readers. Any discussion of this region and its global networks will naturally include discussions of and comparisons to other key areas of the global marketplace. Entrepreneurs and corporations located in or considering entering the Asian market will find the applied empirical examinations of interest. Policymakers and business organizations seeking insight into their own standards and practices can use the data presented to compare their own experiences. Finally, as the recent global crisis has shown, no country or region exists in a vacuum, and the public living in Asia or beyond will benefit from understanding the economic, legal and institutional context of the area before, during and after this momentous two decades. In the following sections, an overview of the issues and summary of the chapters are provided.

1.2 Global Networks and Corporate Governance

Corporate governance is an ubiquitous term, and has been applied to numerous levels of analysis including firm, industry, state and region. Increasingly, with the rise of multinational enterprises and foreign investment, corporate governance applies to a global network of organizations, investors and countries. While there is no universally agreed definition of corporate governance, the term generally refers to the system of management in corporations, and the modes of transparency and accountability that apply to executives, boards, creditors, shareholders, employees and other stakeholders. Naturally, corporate governance is affected by public law, cultural norms, economic development and individual preference. Globalization has thus introduced numerous points of tension regarding corporate governance in developed and developing economies.

Following the Asian crisis, corporate governance was cited as a major contributor of the extent of collapse (ADB, 1999). In fact, there is strong empirical support that corporate governance practices were more directly related to the subsequent declines in currency and equity markets than macroeconomic variables (Stiglitz, 1998; Greenspan, 1999; Johnson and Greening, 1999). Improving macroeconomic policies and conditions leads to the crisis managed to hide weak micro foundations, particularly in the debt management and monitoring practices at the firm level. In Asia, the corporate governance discussions typically involve concentration of ownership, the dependence of executive boards, weak voting rights and family or state control. At the state level, corporate governance is impacted by weak regulatory control and/or corruption. The implications of each individual factor are nonlinear; for example, family ownership may positively impact performance and accountability (Lim *et al.*, 2010).

In the decade between the crises, as the region struggled to correct the failures that precipitated and prolonged the downturn in 1997–1998, corporate governance reform increased. In addition, the strong global economy in the interim between the crises accelerated FDI, and its requisite incentives to improve market governance norms in newly industrialized and emerging economies. Thus, measures like board independence, audit committees and dividend payouts indicate marked improvement in many countries in the region (Sawicki, 2009).

The first section of this volume examines Asian corporate governance from the dual perspectives of norms within the region and as investors in other markets. *En-Te Chen, Stephen Gray* and *John Nowland* (Chapter 2) analyze the issue of family ownership and governance choices in East Asian firms. The authors highlight that new corporate governance standards in many East Asian countries have been introduced between 1999 and 2007, and do not distinguish between ownership type as had historically been the case. The chapter examines the impact of these standards on governance practices in firms of various ownership types. They find that the reformed standards have not caused a convergence of governance norms across ownership types, though the family-owned firms did not always perform worse than other ownership arrangements. The authors make a key contribution by distinguishing between the myriad ownership arrangements in family firms (e.g., founding versus second generation) and non-family firms (e.g., concentrated ownership, government controlled, and company controlled).

Global networks of corporate governance refer to opposite flows of investment as well, namely from Southeast Asia to traditionally developed markets. Indeed, the region has grown individual and institutional investors are increasingly playing roles in corporate governance regimes abroad. For example, the Singapore Central Provident Fund is a significant investor in developed markets, thus acting as principals in foreign corporate ownership.

In the chapter by *Siona Listokin* (Chapter 3), the issue of corporate governance through the proxy access proposals considered in the US by the securities and exchange commission (SEC), which allow shareholders that possess a large ownership stake (in excess of 3% of the firm) for over three years to nominate directors, is described. In the context of these provisions, the chapter also analyses the relationship between ownership of Asian institutional investors and firm value. The chapter assesses the market's reactions to the proxy access provisions. Interestingly, results suggest that Asian (and other non-US) institutional investor ownership does not impact firm value during those times that SEC introduced the provisions. The results support the "passive shareholder" view of large institutional investors, and downplay the policy prescriptions around increasing investor roles in corporate governance.

1.3 Global Networks and Investments

Perhaps the most visible global network involves the flow of funds and resources in and out of developing Asia. This flow can include money, production, labor and technology, and is most easily recognized under the rubric of globalization. The term is obviously widely used in the political and economic discourse about Asia, and it is impossible to briefly define or even introduce the concept (Beeson, 2001). Suffice it is to say, those interested in the globalization phenomena have produced considerable work examining the connection between economic growth, trade and FDI in emerging economies, issues of particular importance in Asia. Discussions of global investment networks frequently involve initial acquisitions, whether of existing entities bought in "fire sales" or in Greenfield projects — distinctions that are vital in the context of the Asian crisis. Less studied, but equally important, are subsequent investments and growth strategies following initial foreign-entry decisions.

Understanding globalization, or overseas investment to and from the region, along with trade (commercial integration) and institutional convergence, is necessary to appreciate changes in Asia — particularly southeast Asia — in the period between the two crises. FDI, trade and integration experienced a rapid acceleration in the pre-Asian crisis period, and again in the years leading up the GFC. However, the nature of these booms were quite different, with a marked increase in intra-Asian trade with China and within the region itself recently (Sakakibara and Yamakawa, 2003). China's growth has also affected foreign investment. Following the 1997–1998 crisis, FDI into the region experienced a considerable decline from the pre-crisis period, and the vast majority of these investments has gone to Singapore and Malaysia; much of the overall regional flow has been redirected to China and India.

The inability within Asia to match pre-crisis levels of global networks and investments has been attributed to many factors, such as weak institutions and the dominance of the Chinese market for global investors. At the same time, intra-regional Asian investment has increased. Financial integration, in turn, has developed in parallel to institutional improvements. Thus, commercial integration (of capital and labor) is linked to market and institutional integration in the region. In the decade between the two crises, integration and investment flows have been mixed; there is a need for more scholarly work in this area.

The second section of the volume aims to bridge some of this gap in empirical work focused on investment and integration. The international business field is replete with studies investigating the firm-specific factors that influence firm-entry decisions, but issues related to governance infrastructure have been largely ignored. Research in the policy field has focused primarily on governance study. *Sonia Ketkar* (Chapter 4) presents a synthesis of these fields in order to explore the post-foreign entry investment and divestment actions of global retail firms in terms of the firm's investment decision in the host market. Ketkar compares the activities of retailers in Asian and non-Asian markets — the aim being to hone in on the developing Asian markets that are constantly in the current news as being the fastest growing regions in the world. The purpose of the comparison is to ascertain whether there are differences in firm investment behavior in Asia. If so, clearly there is a need to probe these differences further. If not, it is possible to contemplate (although certainly not confirm) that foreign firms might be efficient owners of assets in Asia or that, at least in the global retail industry, the decisions to invest in Asia were driven less by the lower asset prices but rather by internal firm factors that were somewhat independent of the time period of the crisis.

In their chapter, *Rabin Hattari, Ramkishen S. Rajan* and *Shandre Thangavelu* (Chapter 5) use bilateral FDI flows data to investigate FDI trends, and the role of macroeconomic, financial and institutional variables in facilitating intra-ASEAN FDI flows over the period from 1990 to 2004. Their chapter also examines the extent and determinants of FDI flows between ASEAN, China and India. Eichengreen and Tong (2007), Liu *et al.* (2007) and Sudsawasd and Chaisrisawatsuk (2006) are three of possibly just a handful of papers that examine FDI to Asia using bilateral data. However, these papers only consider FDI from OECD economies as the source country since they use data from the OECD. In contrast, the focus of this paper is on selected ASEAN economies, India, and China, as both the sources and recipients of FDI, using bilateral FDI data from the United Nations Conference on Trade and Development (UNCTAD). The authors find that a larger host country size, a higher institution quality in the host country, and a greater financial depth in the host country all appear to facilitate bilateral FDI flows within Asia. The policy implications here are apparent. There also appears to be evidence that a shorter distance between countries tends to facilitate bilateral FDI flows.

The chapter by *Tony Cavoli* (Chapter 6) examines some of the salient issues surrounding the degree of economic connections among Asian countries, with particular attention being paid to the nexus between real and financial integrations. Using a novel and simple method, the chapter derives some measures of price-based real and financial integrations from the relative purchasing power parity and uncovered interest parity relationships and then investigates the degree of integration between countries and groups of countries. Generally, it is found that integration is generally higher after the Asian crisis, but the results are quite close. The original ASEAN nations — Indonesia, Malaysia, the Philippines, Singapore and Thailand — seem to be more integrated with rest of Asia than other groups.

Using data and discussion on changes in the geographic origin and industry distribution of large (Top 500) listed companies over the period

2006–2009, *Ron McIver*, (Chapter 7), provides an analysis of the stylized facts and some insight into the conditions, in the context of the relative global position of the East Asian-Pacific region and, more specifically, China. In doing so, it will also address the fact that, while the growth in China's (and, more generally, East Asia's) economic and financial resources and influence are well recognized, there has been less focus on East Asian, and particularly Chinese, control of large multinational corporations as a result of globalization. These large enterprises are important due to their dominance in determining both FDI and trade flows in both directions.

1.4 Global Networks and Macro Policy

The final section of this work extends the analyses of micro-foundations of global networks in Asia (particularly Southeast Asia) to macroeconomic policy. The period after the Asian crisis heralded a number of changes in exchange rate, monetary and financial policy in East Asia, including central bank objectives. Many central banks shifted focus from exchange rates to domestic measures, such as price stability and currency stability (Genberg and He, 2008). For example, Indonesia, South Korea, the Philippines and Thailand unveiled new floating exchange rate systems and/or inflation targets in the past decade (Miyao, 2010). As central banks increasingly emphasize domestic variables like inflation targets, regional cooperation becomes more difficult.

Not surprisingly, given the central banks' renewed focus on domestic economic measures, exchange rates have fluctuated more against the US dollar than they had prior to 1997–1998. In addition, as East Asian trading partners have expanded, their currencies are associated with a wider peg than the US dollar.

Tony Cavoli and Ramkishen S. Rajan (Chapter 8) examine the actual degree of exchange rate flexibility in Asia, following these official changes in policy. Their analysis takes a more detailed look at behavioral exchange rate regimes rather than the typical legal classifications. The results of this in-depth classification and subsequent study point out considerable differences in exchange rate policies among emerging Asian economies, but generally supports greater flexibility of exchange rate regimes and a continued fix to the US dollar.

If more widespread use of inflation targets represents a departure from pre-crisis policies, central bank independence has not followed suit *en masse*. This issue is of central importance because the separation of monetary policy from the daily manipulation of politicians is thought to give credibility to anti-inflationary policies (Rodrik, 2008). Indeed, in regions like Latin America, flexible exchange rates, inflation targets and central bank independence are intimately linked. In Asia, however, few of the central banks are legally independent, though there are exceptions. Nevertheless, the lack of autonomy and a more centralized development strategy has not led to the macroeconomic stability frequently modeled for developing Asia (Bowles and White, 1994).

The volume's final chapter, by *Andrew Hughes-Hallett, Jan Libich and Petr Stehlik* (Chapter 9), addresses the issue of financial stability and monetary policy by creating a model of monetary and fiscal policy under asset bubble conditions. The authors show that first-best policies from politicians and central banks by central bank independence. In cases of dependent central banks, the best policy choice to achieve financial stability involves either the exclusive use of monetary policy (i.e., not fiscal policy) or no policy at all. This is in direct contrast to results under conditions of central bank independence, which allow for a wider range of first-best policy responses. The model has implications for policy responses to the GFC, where it appears that both developed and emerging economies employed inferior policy mixes.

Acknowledgments

We would like to thank the Institute for Southeast Asian Studies for hosting the workshop and all of the participants of the workshop for valuable comments and feedback. The workshop successfully managed to bring together researchers in different fields to address these issues of international business, governance and policy. Also thanks to the Australian Centre for Asian Business at the University of South Australia for financial support and to the Center for Emerging Market Policy at George Mason University. Finally, we wish to thank Belinda Spagnoletti for valuable and competent research assistance during the early stages of the manuscript, and to World Scientific for their support throughout the entire publishing process.

References

Asian Development Bank (ADB) (1999). Corporate governance in East Asia and some policy implications. EDRC Briefing Notes, June.

Beeson, M (2001). Worlds in collision: Southeast Asia and the west. In *The Southeast Asia Handbook*, P Heenan and M Latmontagne (eds.), pp. 231–240. London: Fitzroy-Dearborn.

Bowles, P and G White (1994). Central bank independence: A political economy approach. *J. Dev. Stud.*, 32, 235–264.

Eichengreen, B and H Tong (2007). Is China's FDI coming at the expense of other countries? *J. Jpn. Int. Econ.*, 21, 153–172.

Genberg, H and D He (2008). Monetary and financial cooperation among central banks in East Asia and the Pacific. In *Exchange Rate, Monetary and Financial Issues and Policies in East Asia*, RS Rajan, S Thangavelu and RA Parinduri (eds.), pp. 247–270. Singapore: World Scientific.

Greenspan, A (1999). Do efficient markets mitigate financial crises? Remarks before the 1999 Financial Markets Conference of the Federal Reserve Bank of Atlanta, 19 October, Sea Island, Georgia.

Johnson, RA and DW Greening (1999). The effects of corporate governance and institutional ownership types on corporate social performance. *Acad. Manag. J.*, 42, 564–576.

Lim, ENK, MH Lubatkin and RM Wiseman (2010). A family firm variant of the behavioral agency theory. *Strateg. Entrepreneurship J.*, 4, 197–211.

Liu, L, K Chow and U Li (2007). Determinants of foreign direct investment in East Asia: Did China crowd out FDI from her developing East Asian neighbours? *China World Econ.*, May–June, 70–88.

Miyao, R (2010). Monetary policy and exchange rate stability in East Asia. In *Asian Regionalism in the World Economy: Engine for Dynamism and Stability*, M Kawai, J Lee and P Petri (eds.), pp. 309–358. UK: Edward Elgar Publishing Limited.

Rodrik, D (2008). The real exchange rate and economic growth. *Brookings Pap. on Econ. Activity*, Fall, 365–412.

Sakakibara, E and S Yamakawa (2003). Regional integration in East Asia: challenges and opportunities. World Bank Policy Research Working Paper.

Sawicki, J (2009). Corporate governance and dividend policy in Southeast Asia pre-and post-crisis. *Eur. J. Finance*, 15, 211–230.

Stiglitz, J (1998). Sound finance and sustainable development in Asia. Paper delivered at the Asia Development Forum, Manila, 10–13 March.

Sudsawasd, S and S Chaisrisawatsuk (2006). Tigers and dragons against elephants: Does the rising Chinese and Indian share in trade and foreign direct investment crowd out Thailand and other ASEAN countries? *Asia-Pac. Trade Invest. Rev.*, 2, 93–114.

Part I

Entrepreneurship and Governance

Chapter 2

Convergence in the Ownership and Governance of East Asian Firms

En-Te Chen, Stephen Gray and John Nowland[1]

2.1 Introduction

In the past decade, policymakers in over 70 markets have introduced corporate governance codes or best practice guidelines. In East Asia, they have been introduced in Hong Kong in 1999 and 2006, Indonesia in 2000 and 2007, Malaysia in 2000 and 2007, the Philippines in 2002, Singapore in 2001 and 2005, South Korea in 2003, Taiwan in 2002 and Thailand in 2006. The common focus of these codes is to encourage but not force companies to improve their corporate governance practices to a specified target level, e.g., board independence of 30%. Another commonality is that the guidelines apply to all listed companies regardless of their ownership structure or other characteristics.

Prior to the introduction of these codes, a number of studies documented differences in ownership and governance practices between family and non-family firms.[2] For example, La Porta *et al.* (2002) and Claessens *et al.* (2002) find that the ownership of family firms is generally more complex, involving dual-class shares, cross-holdings and pyramid ownership structures, which result in greater control rights than cashflow rights. Anderson and Reeb (2004) and Yeh and Woidtke (2005) show that family owners

[1]The authors would like to thank Cindy Peng for excellent research assistance and acknowledge the financial support of an AFAANZ research grant 2008–2009 and City University of Hong Kong new staff grant.
[2]Family firms are specifically identified as they are the dominant form of corporate ownership around the world, comprising an average of 59% of listed firms in Asia (ex-Japan) and 44% in Europe (Claessens *et al.*, 2000; Faccio and Lang, 2002).

tend to dominate the board of directors. Both of these phenomena result in high agency costs between the family group and other shareholders and are associated with lower firm performance.

The main focus of corporate governance regulation is to improve governance practices and thereby reduce agency conflicts within firms. This assumes that the ownership and governance practices of firms are not at their value-maximizing optimum. For example, the weaker governance practices of family firms are the result of family owners seeking to increase their private benefits of control and are not in the best interests of other shareholders. Recent studies have confirmed that this is the case by finding that improvements in the corporate governance practices of firms, particularly family firms, are associated with improved performance (Dahya *et al.*, 2008; Nowland, 2008).

The contribution of this study is to examine whether the ownership and governance practices of East Asian firms have converged since the introduction of corporate governance codes. Consistent with previous research, we compare the ownership and governance of family firms to non-family firms. We then extend the analysis in two ways. First, we compare family firms to various categories of non-family firms (individual-controlled, government-controlled, company-controlled and widely-held). This approach recognizes the heterogeneity of non-family firms and allows for a better comparison of family firms to other firms with similar ownership characteristics. Second, we recognize the heterogeneity of family firms and differentiate between family firms that were founded and acquired by family owners, and family firms that are in their first and second generations of family control.

Our main analysis uses data from all listed companies on the Taiwan Stock Exchange in 2007.[3] Our results indicate that family firms continue to maintain higher board representation and lower board independence than most other firms. However, we do not find that agency problems related to ownership and governance practices are always greatest in family firms.

---

[3]We use data from Taiwan as listed companies disclose both their ownership structure and board of director relationships. Our analysis is also supplemented by data from six other East Asian markets.

We find that the board governance practices of family firms sit between those of individual-controlled and government-controlled firms. Examining differences among family firms, we find that acquired family firms are owned differently but governed the same as founded family firms and that second-generation family firms have a higher control wedge, higher board representation and lower board independence than first-generation family firms. We find the differences between first- and second-generation family firms encouraging as they show that family firms are evolving towards less control-enhancing ownership structures and more independent boards of directors. However, overall our results show that ownership and governance choices continue to differ between firms depending on the identity and generation of the controlling owner. We discuss policy implications in the conclusions.

2.2 Data and Variables

Our main sample comprises 718 firms in the Taiwan Stock Exchange that provided annual reports to the exchange for the year 2007 and have financial and ownership data available from the *Taiwan Economic Journal* (TEJ) database. We identify the original founders of the sample firms by analyzing annual reports, company websites and internet searches. We then manually check annual reports of all firms to identify who occupies each of the board seats, their family connections and the firms they represent, and the number of independent directors and supervisors on the board. We categorize firms into family-controlled, individual-controlled, government-controlled, company-controlled and widely-held using the following methodology. If a particular group (family, individual, government, and company) holds more board seats (including seats held directly and through representatives) than any other group then they are deemed to be in control. If two groups hold an equal number of board seats then the group deemed to be in control is the one who founded the firm, and if there is no founder, the group who holds the Chairman position. If no group holds more than one board seat then the firm is categorized as widely-held. We do not impose minimum ownership restrictions as we view ownership as a vehicle to obtain representation on the board of directors. Where our ownership categorizations differ from the TEJ database, we recalculate ownership variables.

Individual-controlled firms differ from family-controlled firms in that they are controlled by a single person with no involvement from other family members. In company-controlled firms, the controlling group is a firm whose ownership cannot be traced to a family, individual or government controlling shareholder. Family firms are also further classified as founded family firms, acquired family firms, first-generation family firms and second-generation family firms. In founded family firms, the controlling group is the same family that originally founded the firm. In acquired family firms, the controlling group is a family who has acquired the firm after it was founded. First-generation family firms are founded family firms where the original founder is still involved on the board of directors. Second-generation family firms are founded family firms where the original founder is no longer involved but one or more of their descendents is on the board of directors.

Of the 718 sample firms, 536 are classified as family-controlled firms, 109 as individual-controlled firms, 25 as government-controlled firms, 34 as company-controlled firms and 12 as widely-held firms. Within the family-controlled firms, 448 are founded family firms and 88 are acquired family firms. Of the founded family firms, 288 are first-generation family firms and 160 are second-generation family firms.

In our subsequent analysis, we examine differences in the following variables. Ownership variables are calculated following the methodology of Claessens *et al.* (2000). *Ultimate ownership* is the cash flow rights ownership of the controlling owner. *Control wedge* is the ratio of control to cash flow rights of the controlling owner. *Board size* is the total number of directors and supervisors. *Board representation* is the number of controlling owner representative directors and supervisors as a percentage of board size. *Board independence* is the number of independent directors and supervisors as a percentage of board size. *Chairman–CEO duality* is a dummy variable equal to one when the same person holds both positions. *Total assets* are our measure of firm size, which is displayed in billions of NT dollars. *Age* is the number of years since the firm was founded. *Tobin's Q* is the market value of assets divided by the book value of assets. *Return on assets* is earnings before interest and tax divided by total assets.

2.3 Empirical Results

2.3.1 *Family versus non-family firms*

In Table 2.1, we follow the methodology of previous research and compare family firms with non-family firms.[4] Comparing the ownership variables, we find that family firms have higher ultimate ownership than non-family firms.

Table 2.1.　Family versus Non-Family Firms.

	(1) Family Firms ($n = 536$)	(2) Non-Family Firms ($n = 182$)	(1)–(2) t-statistics
Ultimate ownership (%)	24.79	17.39	5.19***
Control wedge	1.55	1.67	−0.71
Board size	9.88	10.23	−1.37
Board representation (%)	51.49	36.89	6.94***
Board independence (%)	9.27	16.26	−5.62***
Chairman–CEO duality (%)	31.72	38.33	−1.59
Total assets (NT$ billions)	30.27	28.16	0.25
Age	29.02	21.18	6.93***
Tobin's Q	1.18	1.17	0.26
Return on assets	9.19	11.41	−1.14

Note: Table displays mean values for family and non-family firms. Firms with a family group holding the largest number of board seats are classified as family firms. The sample includes 718 firms listed in the Taiwan Stock Exchange in 2007. Data is from the TEJ database and company annual reports. Asterisks denote significance of mean t-tests as follows: *10%, **5%, and ***1%.

---

[4]For simplicity, we present results of means tests. Results are consistent using regressions which control for differences in additional firm characteristics such as firm size, age, leverage, growth, past performance and industry factors. Results are also consistent if we remove financial firms from the sample.

This is expected as non-family firms also include widely-held firms, where this is no obvious controlling shareholder. In contrast to previous research, we find no significant difference in the size of the control wedge between family and non-family firms. This is most likely due to our categorization of individual-controlled firms as non-family firms, whereas previous research has generally bundled them together with family firms (Miller *et al.*, 2007). Examining the board of director variables, we find that family firms have higher board representation and lower board independence than non-family firms. There is no significant difference in board size and the incidence of Chairman–CEO duality. This is consistent with prior research and suggests that family firms continue to maintain higher board representation and lower board independence, even though these variables have been highlighted as associated with higher agency problems and lower firm value (Dahya *et al.*, 2008; Yeh and Woidtke, 2005).

As an additional test of the board governance practices of firms, we examine the percentage of firms that have adopted the Taiwan Corporate Governance code recommendations of two independent directors and one independent supervisor on their boards. This is particularly interesting as firms in Taiwan could not legally have independent directors and supervisors prior to 2001. This means all firms started from the same base and we can clearly see which firms have made more progress. The results are displayed in Fig. 2.1 and show that 50% of non-family firms have two independent directors on their boards compared to 28% of family firms. In addition, 38% of non-family firms have one independent supervisor on their boards, compared to 20% of family firms. These results confirm that differences exist in the board governance practices of family firms relative to non-family firms.

Since our analysis has so far centered on our sample of firms from Taiwan, it is possible that the same trends are not occurring in other Asian markets. To overcome this concern, we provide some results from Nowland (2008), who examined the board independence of 221 firms from seven East Asian countries over the period 1998–2004. The countries are Hong Kong, Indonesia, Malaysia, the Philippines, Singapore, Thailand and Taiwan. Figure 2.2 shows the trends in board independence for family firms and non-family firms over the period. The results show that the board independence of all firms has increased over the period, but there is no evidence

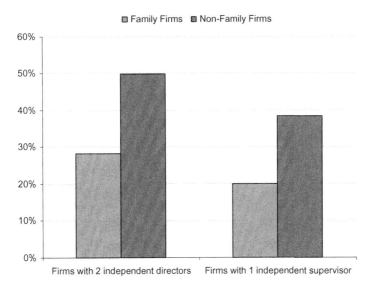

Fig. 2.1.   Percentage of Firms Meeting Taiwan Corporate Governance Code Board Independence Guidelines.

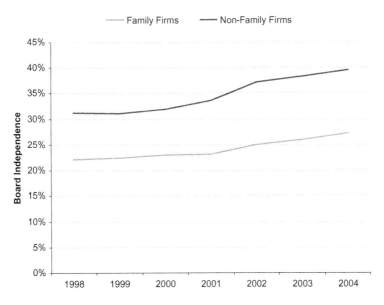

Fig. 2.2.   Board Independence of 221 Firms from Seven East Asian Countries 1998–2004.
Source: Nowland (2008).

that the board independence of family firms is converging to that of non-family firms. This confirms that the results of our analysis are unlikely to be specific to Taiwan, as there is no evidence of convergence in firms from other East Asian markets.

2.3.2 *Family versus other firm types*

In Table 2.2, we extend our analysis by differentiating between the various types of non-family firms (individual-controlled, government-controlled, company-controlled and widely-held). This approach recognizes the heterogeneity of non-family firms and allows for a better comparison of family firms to other firms with similar ownership characteristics. Comparing family firms with widely-held firms we find identical results to those in the previous section. Family firms have higher ultimate ownership, higher board representation and lower board independence. However, comparing family firms with firms that have no identifiable controlling owner is not a good match. We therefore turn our attention to comparing family firms with individual-controlled, government-controlled and company-controlled firms.

Comparing family firms with individual-controlled firms we find that family firms have higher ultimate ownership, a lower control wedge, bigger boards, higher board representation, lower board independence and a lower incidence of Chairman–CEO duality. Family firms are also older and have lower returns on assets than individual-controlled firms. These results suggest that the ownership structure of individual-controlled firms is more of a concern than that of family firms as they have both lower ultimate ownership and a higher control wedge. However, this is offset by the board governance practices of individual-controlled firms, who have less board representation from the individual owner and higher board independence. Higher Chairman–CEO duality in individual-controlled firms suggests that the individual is more likely to hold both positions than a particular family member. Overall, these results are consistent with Miller *et al.* (2007) who show that individual-controlled firms are different and perform better than family firms.

Comparing family firms to government-controlled firms we find that there are no significant differences in ownership characteristics, but family

Table 2.2. Family Firms versus Other Firm Types.

	(1) Family Firms (n = 536)	(2) Widely-held Firms (n = 12)	(3) Individual Firms (n = 109)	(4) Government Firms (n = 25)	(5) Company Firms (n = 34)	(1)–(2) t-statistics	(1)–(3) t-statistics	(1)–(4) t-statistics	(1)–(5) t-statistics
Ultimate ownership (%)	24.79	9.10	13.19	27.42	25.48	3.18***	6.73***	−0.76	−0.23
Control wedge	1.55	1.00	2.00	1.33	1.00	1.42	−2.19**	0.82	2.38***
Board size	9.88	9.75	9.39	14.12	10.06	0.15	1.69*	−6.83***	−0.35
Board representation (%)	51.49	10.51	30.98	62.82	46.08	5.81***	8.21***	−2.27**	1.26
Board independence (%)	9.27	18.10	21.39	4.13	9.03	−2.19**	−8.07***	1.84*	0.10
Chairman–CEO duality (%)	31.72	33.33	46.79	8.00	35.29	−0.12	−3.04***	2.52***	−0.43
Total assets (NT$ billions)	30.27	29.04	28.36	51.87	11.11	0.04	0.18	−1.01	1.06
Age	29.02	21.75	17.45	27.88	28.06	1.88*	8.72***	0.41	0.41
Tobin's Q	1.18	1.09	1.19	1.19	1.11	0.81	−0.29	−0.05	1.07
Return on assets	9.19	8.68	14.99	8.82	2.85	0.11	−3.11***	0.11	2.16**

Note: Table displays mean values for family, widely-held, individual-controlled, government-controlled and company-controlled firms. Firms with a family group/individual/government/company holding the largest number of board seats are classified as family/individual/government/company firms. Widely-held firms are those where no individual or group holds more than one board seat. Ultimate ownership is the cashflow rights ownership of the controlling owner. Control wedge is the ratio of control to cashflow rights of the controlling owner. Board size is the number of directors and supervisors. Board representation is the number of controlling owner representative directors and supervisors as a percentage of board size. Board independence is the number of independent directors and supervisors as a percentage of board size. Chairman–CEO duality is a dummy variable equal to one when the same person holds both positions. Total assets are in billions of NT dollars. Age is the number of years since the firm was founded. Tobin's Q is the market value of assets divided by the book value of assets. Return on assets is earnings before interest and tax divided by total assets. The sample includes 718 firms listed in the Taiwan Stock Exchange in 2007. Data is from the TEJ database and company annual reports. Asterisks denote significance of mean t-tests as follows: * 10%, ** 5%, and *** 1%.

firms have smaller boards, lower board representation, higher board independence and a higher incidence of Chairman–CEO duality. These results
indicate that the board governance practices of government-controlled firms
(higher board representation and lower board independence) are more of an
agency concern that those of family firms. The final comparison between
family firms and company-controlled firms shows few significant differences. Family firms maintain a higher control wedge and have higher return
on assets than company-controlled firms. There are no significant differences in their board governance practices.

Overall, the results from this section show that there are considerable differences across firm types. Family firms have often been singled
out by previous research as being different from other firms. However,
further examination of non-family firms shows that there are differences between individual-controlled, government-controlled, company-
controlled and widely-held firms. In particular, the results indicate that the
board governance practices of family firms are between those of individual-
controlled and government-controlled firms. We do not find that agency
problems related to ownership and governance practices are always greatest
in family firms.

2.3.3 *Founded versus acquired family firms*

In this section, we separate family firms according to whether they have
been founded or acquired by the controlling family group. Founded family
firms are those where the same family group has been in control of the
firm since its founding. This means that the family has had the freedom to
establish their desired ownership and governance practices. Acquired family
firms were not founded but have been acquired by the current controlling
family group sometime during their existence. This means their ownership
and governance practices will be shaped by both the original founders, the
circumstances in which the current family group purchased the firm, and
the governance preferences of the current family group.

Table 2.3 displays the differences between founded and acquired family
firms. We find that founded family firms have higher ultimate ownership and
a lower control wedge than acquired family firms. There are no significant
differences in the board of director variables or other firm characteristics.
The ownership results indicate that acquired family firms are more likely to

Table 2.3.   Founded versus Acquired Family Firms.

	(1) Founded Family Firms ($n = 448$)	(2) Acquired Family Firms ($n = 88$)	(1)–(2) t-statistics
Ultimate ownership (%)	25.69	20.16	2.80***
Control wedge	1.47	1.99	−3.35***
Board size	9.82	10.16	−0.99
Board representation (%)	51.60	50.93	0.24
Board independence (%)	9.30	9.07	0.14
Chairman–CEO duality (%)	33.04	25.00	1.48
Total assets (NT$ billions)	31.59	23.55	0.65
Age	28.95	29.41	−0.30
Tobin's Q	1.18	1.18	−0.04
Return on assets	9.62	7.01	1.42

Note: Table displays mean values for founded and acquired family firms. Firms where the family group that founded the firm holds the largest number of board seats that are classified as founded family firms. Firms, where a family group that did not find the firm holding the largest number of board seats, are classified as acquired family firms. Ultimate ownership is the cashflow rights ownership of the controlling owner. Control wedge is the ratio of control to cashflow rights of the controlling owner. Board size is the number of directors and supervisors. Board representation is the number of controlling owner representative directors and supervisors as a percentage of board size. Board independence is the number of independent directors and supervisors as a percentage of board size. Chairman–CEO duality is a dummy variable equal to one when the same person holds both positions. Total assets are in billions of NT dollars. Age is the number of years since the firm was founded. Tobin's Q is the market value of assets divided by the book value of assets. Return on assets is earnings before interest and tax divided by total assets. The sample includes 718 firms listed in the Taiwan Stock Exchange in 2007. Data is from the TEJ database and company annual reports. Asterisks denote significance of mean t-tests as follows: *10%, **5%, and ***1%.

be owned at the lower levels of pyramid ownership structures, which results in lower ultimate ownership by the family group and a higher control wedge. The board of director results show that even though the firms were not founded by the family group, they have adopted board governance practices that are consistent with their other firms. In summary, the results show that acquired family firms are owned differently but governed in the same way as founded family firms.

2.3.4   First- versus second-generation family firms

In this section, we distinguish between founded family firms that are in their first and second generations of family control. First-generation family firms are founded family firms where the original founder is still on the board of directors. Second-generation family firms are founded family firms where the original founder is no longer on the board but one or more of their descendents are. We expect differences between these two types of family firms due to two factors. First, previous research has shown that first-generation family firms perform better because they are still under the leadership of the original founder (Villalonga and Amit, 2006). Second, if the ownership and governance practices of family firms are changing over time then first-generation family firms, which were founded more recently, are more likely to display characteristics of more recent practices.

Table 2.4 shows the differences between first- and second-generation family firms. We find that there is no difference in ultimate ownership, but that second-generation family firms have a higher control wedge. Second-generation family firms also have bigger boards, higher board representation and lower board independence than first-generation family firms. First-generation family firms have a higher incidence of Chairman–CEO duality, which reflects the dual role played by the company founder. As expected, first-generation family firms are younger and have higher return on assets than second-generation family firms. These results indicate that the ownership structure of family firms is changing over time, with first-generation family firms relying less on control-enhancing structures. The board governance practices of first-generation family firms also appear to be associated with lower agency problems (lower board representation and higher board independence).

2.4   Conclusions

Over the past decade, corporate governance policies around the world have prescribed the same guidelines for all types of firms. This is at odds with the academic literature which has found significant differences between firm types (e.g., between family and non-family firms). We examine whether the ownership and governance practices of East Asian family firms have converged to those of non-family firms, as prescribed by corporate governance

Table 2.4.   First- versus Second-Generation Family Firms.

	(1) First-Generation Family Firms ($n = 288$)	(2) Second-Generation Family Firms ($n = 160$)	(1)–(2) t-statistics
Ultimate ownership (%)	25.99	25.16	0.50
Control wedge	1.26	1.83	−5.09***
Board size	9.47	10.46	−3.48***
Board representation (%)	45.63	62.34	−7.27***
Board independence (%)	10.89	6.44	3.29***
Chairman–CEO duality (%)	40.28	20.00	4.46***
Total assets (NT$ billions)	26.25	41.20	−1.39
Age	26.30	33.73	−6.15***
Tobin's Q	1.18	1.19	−0.37
Return on assets	10.99	7.14	2.65***

Note: Table displays mean values for first- and second-generation family firms. Firms, where the family group that founded the firm, hold the largest number of board seats and the founder is still involved as a director are classified as first-generation family firms. Firms where the family group that founded the firm hold the largest number of board seats and the founder is no longer involved but the founder's descendents are involved in the firm are classified as second-generation family firms. Ultimate ownership is the cashflow rights ownership of the controlling owner. Control wedge is the ratio of control to cashflow rights of the controlling owner. Board size is the number of directors and supervisors. Board representation is the number of controlling owner representative directors and supervisors as a percentage of board size. Board independence is the number of independent directors and supervisors as a percentage of board size. Chairman–CEO duality is a dummy variable equal to one when the same person holds both positions. Total assets are in billions of NT dollars. Age is the number of years since the firm was founded. Tobin's Q is the market value of assets divided by the book value of assets. Return on assets is earnings before interest and tax divided by total assets. The sample includes 718 firms listed in the Taiwan Stock Exchange in 2007. Data is from the TEJ database and company annual reports. Asterisks denote significance of mean t-tests as follows: *10%, **5%, and ***1%.

policies. Following the methodology of previous research, we compare family and non-family firms and find that family firms continue to maintain higher board representation and lower board independence, even though these characteristics have been associated with higher agency problems in the academic literature. To show that this trend is not limited to our sample of firms from Taiwan, we also present results from seven Asian markets, which show that the board independence of family firms is not converging to that of non-family firms.

However, since this approach does not recognize the heterogeneity of non-family firms, we undertake further analysis by comparing family firms to various categories of non-family firms (individual-controlled, government-controlled, company-controlled and widely-held). We find that there are considerable differences between individual-controlled, government-controlled, company-controlled and widely-held firms. In particular, the results indicate that the board governance practices of family firms are between those of individual-controlled and government-controlled firms. We do not find that agency problems related to ownership and governance practices are always greatest in family firms. We also recognize the heterogeneity of family firms and differentiate between family firms that were founded and acquired by family owners, and family firms that are in their first and second generations of family control. We find that acquired family firms are owned differently but governed the same as founded family firms and that second-generation family firms have a higher control wedge, higher board representation and lower board independence than first-generation family firms.

The results indicate that ownership and governance choices continue to differ between firms depending on the identity and generation of the controlling owner, most likely because these structures are persistent and costly to alter over time. However, there is some evidence that ownership structures are evolving with first-generation family firms relying less on control-enhancing structures than second-generation family firms. With respect to board governance practices, we find considerable variation across different firm types, which suggests that current corporate governance policies have done little to bring about convergence in practices. Figure 2.3 displays the average board representation and board independence of the different firm types identified in this study. From an agency cost perspective, the firms requiring more emphasis on corporate governance are second-generation family firms and government-controlled firms.

For policymakers, our analysis indicates that voluntary corporate governance codes have not been successful in encouraging the convergence of ownership and governance practices across firms. Some policy suggestions for the future include setting mandatory lower bounds on board

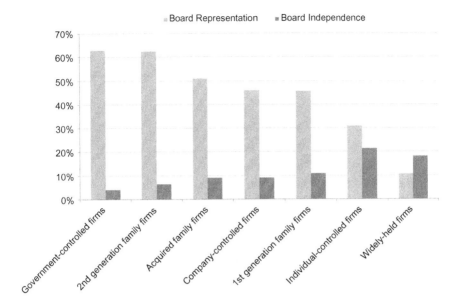

Fig. 2.3.   Board Representation and Independence by Firm Type.

independence and mandatory upper limits on board representation (equal to ownership rights). This will help to minimize the variation across firms around the specified target. Our analysis also shows that it would be possible to customize recommendations across a small number of identifiable sub-groups of firms, e.g., family firms, individual-controlled firms, government-controlled firms and widely-held firms, rather than using one set of recommendations for all firms.

References

Anderson, R and D Reeb (2004). Board composition: Balancing family influence in S&P500 firms. *Admin. Sci. Q.*, 49, 209–237.

Claessens, S, S Djankov and L Lang (2000). The separation of ownership and control in East Asian corporations. *J. Financial Econ.*, 58, 81–112.

Claessens, S, S Djankov, J Fan and L Lang (2002). Disentangling the incentive and entrenchment effects of large shareholdings. *J. Finance*, 57, 2741–2772.

Dahya, J, O Dimitrov and J McConnell (2008). Dominant shareholders, corporate boards and corporate value: A cross-country analysis. *J. Financial Econ.*, 87, 73–100.

Faccio, M and L Lang (2002). The ultimate ownership of Western European corporations. *J. Financial Econ.*, 65, 365–395.

La Porta, R, F López De Silanes, A Shleifer and R Vishny (2002). Investor protection and corporate valuation. *J. Finance*, 57, 1147–1170.

Miller, D, I Le Breton-Miller, R Lester and A Cannella (2007). Are family firms really superior performers? *J. Corp. Finance*, 13, 829–858.

Nowland, J (2008). Are East Asian companies benefiting from western board practices? *J. Bus. Ethics*, 79, 133–150.

Villalonga, B and R Amit (2006). How do family ownership, management and control affect firm value? *J. Financial Econ.*, 80, 385–417.

Yeh, YH and T Woidtke (2005). Commitment of entrenchment?: Controlling shareholders and board composition. *J. Bank. Finance*, 29, 1857–1885.

Chapter 3

Asian and Non-Asian Institutional Investors and Proxy Access Proposals

Siona Listokin

3.1 Introduction

Globalizing equity markets has increased firms' access to capital while diversifying investment (Dahlquist and Robertsson, 2001). At the same time, ownership within countries has been transformed by the rise of institutional investors (Black, 1992). These dual changes have given rise to questions regarding the impact of foreign and institutional investor ownership on firm value and behavior, especially following the failure of corporate governance in the 2007–2008 financial crisis (Steverman and Bogoslaw, 2008). The issue of effective shareholder monitoring lends itself to specific questions about which shareholders are value-maximizing watchdogs of corporate management, and how public policy can improve these owners' ability to monitor the firm.

This chapter examines one policy response in the United States to improve corporate governance by increasing shareholders' ability to nominate directors to the corporate board on shareholder proxy forms; proxy access proposals have been considered in Congress, the Securities and Exchange Commission (SEC) and in state legislatures. In August 2010, the SEC adopted new proxy access rules allowing shareholders with a large ownership stake — over 3% of the firm and held for a period of at least three years — the ability to nominate directors.

It is unclear if proxy access would improve firm value. Most proxy access proposals are limited to shareholders with significant ownership stakes, which typically includes certain individuals with a tie to the firm and large institutional investors. Principal–agent theory predicts that large shareholders have particular incentives and cost advantages to monitor management, and giving them increased control over the corporate board will improve shareholder value (Admati *et al.*, 1994). More recently, theories of "agency capitalism" note that principles in the form of institutional investors are themselves agents and may not be acting to maximize long-term shareholder value (Gilson, 2007; Strine Jr, 2007). Empowering these institutional investors via proxy nominations to the corporate board may in fact be detrimental to the firm.

Studies have analyzed the relationship between institutional investor ownership and firm value, volatility, corporate governance, strategy and social responsibility, with little consensus (Demsetz and Villalonga, 2001; Gillan and Starks, 2000; Hotchkiss and Strickland, 2003; Smith, 1996; Chhibber and Majumdar, 1999; Kotter and Lel, 2008). A key issue involves the composition and internationalization of institutional investor ownership, which could include mutual funds, hedge funds, pension funds, sovereign wealth funds and other types with varying political, economic and social motivations. In studies that distinguish between institutional investor types, public pension funds and sovereign wealth funds are frequently differentiated based on their investment priorities and political issues (Johnson and Greening, 1999; Qui, 2003; Romano, 1993; Woidtke, 2002; Kotter and Lel, 2008). In this area, too, there is no empirical consensus as to whether "activist" or government-owned institutional investors like public pension funds are beneficial to the firm.

There is no consensus about how particular classes of foreign investors may influence corporate governance in the US. Specifically, the behavior of Asian institutional investors is understudied. Previous work notes that activist investor groups have formed in Asia, but the effect of these developments on non-Asian (or in this case, the US) equity markets is unknown (Gillan and Starks, 2003).

The results of this chapter suggest that large institutional investors play a role in the impacts of opening proxy access, as measured by market reaction. When differentiated from domestic owners, foreign institutional investors do not appear to have an economically significant effect on firm value. The chapter uses event study methodology involving proxy access proposals made by the SEC since 2002.

This study directly measures the relationship between firm value and Asian institutional ownership composition, in contrast to a number of papers that examine intermediate variables. For example, Almazan *et al.* (2005) examine ownership composition and executive composition. Johnson and Greening (1999) examine the relationship between institutional investor composition and corporate governance. While there are limitations using market value for firm valuation (Demsetz and Villalonga, 2001) the examples cited here point to intermediating variables that can confound the issue.

Other work in this area suffers from threats to internal validity, most notably endogeneity — after all, ownership decisions are not random. Other papers have dealt with this issue by lagging variables or using a large number of firm control variables (Demsetz and Lehn, 1985; Woidtke, 2002). This study most closely resembles Larcker *et al.*'s (2010) paper looking at SEC, congressional and state corporate governance policy events since 2007. This analysis does not distinguish between foreign and domestic institutional investors, and is interested in a number of corporate governance variables in addition to proxy access and ownership. In addition, this study builds upon an earlier paper (Listokin, 2012) that examines the importance of distinguishing between investor types, though Asian governance issues are not included.

In addition, this study contributes to the growing perspective in the governance literature on agency capitalism in an era of shifting and increasingly globalized owners. The results underscore that distinguishing between investor types' matters, and region matters. While this study distinguishes between foreign — in particular, Pacific region — and domestic institutional investors, the growth of activist investors such as hedge funds and private equity funds may produce very different results (2008).

3.2 Institutional Investors

Institutional investors own an increasing share of public corporations, growing from 10% in the 1950s to over 70% recently (Gillan and Starks, 2007). As institutional investors' ownership has increased in prominence, interest in their influence on public corporations has grown as well. The effect of institutional ownership on factors such as firm performance, market value, volatility and corporate governance is frequently studied, often with ambiguous results (Gillan and Starks, 2000). Scholars (Admati *et al.*, 1994; Black, 1992; Jensen and Meckling, 1976; Shleifer and Vishny, 1986) argue that institutional investors have large shareholder stakes in firms and can develop informational advantages. These factors can reduce the agency problem between managers and owners by increasing firm value.

Empirical research, however, is far from conclusive (Del Guercio and Hawkins, 1999; Gillan and Starks, 2000; Hotchkiss and Strickland, 2003; McConnell and Servaes, 1990; Smith, 1996; Wahal, 2009). Early empirical studies failed to differentiate among various types of institutional investors, which may have diluted results. Pension funds, mutual funds, and other investment firms have diverse stakeholders themselves and different investment criteria (Neubam and Zahra, 2006). This duality can mitigate the monitoring function ascribed to institutional investors. Agency capitalism is skeptical of the traditional principle-agent model, in that institutional investors may not use their substantial ownership stake to maximize long-term value, rather than maximize more immediate agent concerns (Gilson, 2007; Gordon, 2008; Pollock, 2007; Strine Jr, 2007). Such "myopic institutions" are short sighted in response to the short-term performance metrics that determine compensation and advancement (Hansen and Hill, 1991). Empowering institutional investors may not serve the role of enabling principal shareholders — a diffuse group of individuals contending with dual agency issues with their fund manager and investment executives — with an effective voice (Pollock, 2007; Strine Jr, 2007).

Investors can influence management through a variety of channels, including shareholder proposals, director nominations with proxy access and access to management. Shareholder proposals may serve functions that differ from pressurizing management; communication between significant shareholders and management can take place outside of the formal process through direct contact (Gordon, 2008). Shareholder proposals may be one of the means of communicating the intentions of the owners to the general public rather than a declaration of intent or threat (David *et al.*, 2007; Black, 1992). Shareholder resolutions under SEC Rule 14a-8 are dominated by special interest groups, such as religious, union or public pension fund investors (Chandler, 1999).

Proxy access refers to the ability to include shareholder-nominated board directors on the company proxy statement. While shareholders can nominate directors without proxy access, it is prohibitively expensive to wage a realistic campaign, resulting in few outside challenges to the corporate board (Bebchuk, 2003; Pozen, 2003). Recent corporate governance reforms' proposals have considered revising proxy access to allow large qualified shareholders (defined variably as 1% to 5% owners, frequently with a minimum ownership tenure), or clusters of smaller qualified shareholders, to include nominees in the proxy materials; The aim of these requirements is to screen nominations and allow only those whose support among shareholders is reasonable. (Bebchuk, 2003).

Reforms to the proxy access process have been proposed at the SEC three times since 2003 (2003, 2007 and 2009) (SEC, 2009). The three reform ideas varied in specifics, but shared elements regarding threshold sizes and ownership tenure required for proxy access. In the 2003 proposals, proxy access would be contingent on certain "triggering events"; the proposal faded after initiating an active response (see the SEC Summary of Comments released July 15, 2003). In 2007, following a Second Circuit Court decision that opened shareholder changes of bylaws granting proxy access (AFSCME versus AIG, 2d Cir. 2006), the SEC again proposed a version of proxy access, but failed to take final action on the relevant proposals. The SEC revisited the issue next in 2009, and finally adopted a proposal on August 25, 2010.

A robust debate followed the failed reforms. Bebchuk (2003, 2007) proposes that proxy access provides shareholders with "an important safety valve" to remove or influence directors regarding issues such as compensation, acquisitions and risk management. Without proxy access, corporate directors are rarely challenged in shareholder elections, rendering the directors' incentives to act in shareholders' best interests (rather than management's) too weak. In such cases, management may be able to extract rents from shareholders, through avenues such as compensation or risk-taking.

On the other side of the debate, scholars argue that the "safety valve" argument relies on the assumptions that qualifying shareholders know what is in the best interests of the firm and that they do not have other, possibly conflicting special interests. According to Pozen (2003), public pension funds may be exceptional in that their institutional interests may be political rather than purely financial (Pozen, 2003; Romano, 2003). In this case, directors nominated by large public pension fund shareholders could decrease firm value with minority support. Another example includes hedge funds interested in short-term profits and high volatility (Chandler, 1999). Other arguments against proxy access include increased cost due to elections and director distraction, balkanization of the board and unnecessary costs of regulation (especially in the case of federal government proposals).

These competing views have been labeled as rent extraction versus value maximizing (Larcker *et al.*, 2010). The first predicts that since management is extracting rents from shareholders' absent proxy access, increasing the probability of proxy access would increase value based on the level of institutional investment. The latter holds that current practice maximizes value, and proxy access proposals are predicted to have negative effects based on ownership. The first hypothesis predicts the rent extraction force is more prevalent.

*H*1: Large institutional investor ownership increases firm value when proxy access is more probable.

Foreign investors own about 12% of the US corporate stocks (Jackson, 2008). The US benefits from these inflows in that corporations have greater financial flexibility and can increase their knowledge flows. Likewise, foreign investors benefit from high risk-return ratios (generally), strong corporate governance institutions and stability. Like their domestic counterparts, foreign institutional investors — made up of investment funds, pension funds, sovereign wealth funds and other types — are frequently looking to the medium or long-term, and can be passive investors. These factors, along with the exchange rate risk, can make some types of foreign institutional investors excellent sources of equity capital for corporations (Dimelis and Louri, 2002).

Large foreign institutional investors can target firms for investment, indicating a strategic interest in the corporation beyond its place in an investment portfolio (GPFG, 2009; Kotter and Lel, 2008). Thus, foreign investors may serve as more effective firm monitors than their domestic counterparts. On the other hand, such targeted investment may have interests outside of value-maximization, making foreign investor engagement a negative factor for firm value.

Asian institutional investors include some of the largest investment funds in the world, such as the Japan Government Pension Investment Trust (Listokin, 2011). While there is little academic literature on Asian institutional investor behavior in the US equity markets, there is support for the characterization of a passive investment strategy in the region (Aronson, 2005; Han, 2003). This type of passive investment would be predicted to moderate the impact of proxy access rule changes.

*H*2: Large foreign institutional investor ownership increases firm when proxy access is more probable.

*H*3: Large Asian institutional investor ownership does not impact firm value when proxy access is more probable.

3.3 Data and Research Methods

3.3.1 *Sample and data*

This study examines market reactions to five events involving proposals to change proxy access rules. Major proxy access events are identified by searching for instances of "proxy", "director" and "14a" (to correspond to Section 14(a) of the SEC) in the SEC press releases from 1999–2010. These events are further screened for events relating to proxy access (for example, announcements related to "e-proxy" rules are omitted), and for releases that mark a novel development rather than continue consideration of changing proxy access rules. For example, announcements related to solicitation of public views regarding possible changes are omitted. In addition, press releases concerning action against specific entities based on proxy procedures or related to disclosure of proxy voting policy within institutional funds are not included. The list of events is cross-referenced with a Lexis–Nexis search of *The New York Times* and *Wall Street Journal* to determine the first date that possible rule changes are publicly indicated. For example, the 2009 cycle of proxy access proposals began in May 20, 2009, but both newspapers carried the news datelined the previous day. The five significant proxy events are listed in Table 3.1.

The dependent variable is the firm abnormal stock return, over the CRSP value-weighted market index. Abnormal returns controls for firm betas in addition to covariance between firms (Campbell *et al.*, 1997). The variable

Table 3.1.   Proxy Access Announcement Dates.

Date	Event
April 14, 2003	SEC announces commission to review current proxy rules and regulations to improve corporate democracy.
September 30, 2003	Commission officials said that SEC would approve new rules on proxy access, according to quotes in *The New York Times*. Large shareholders can nominate up to three directors for large boards. The rule includes triggering events, setting up a two-stage process for nomination.
April 24, 2007	SEC announces round table discussions regarding proxy process, following court decisions that may have resulted in uncertainty regarding shareholder proposals about board elections.
July 26, 2007	SEC announces plan to solicit comments on proposed amendments on proxy access, after a 3–2 vote. The proposal text was not immediately released.
May 20, 2009	SEC votes to propose rule amendments to facilitate rights of shareholders to nominate directors. The proposal requires that shareholders own at least 1–5% of the company's securities (depending on the investor type) for at least one year to meet requirements to nominate a director in the company's proxy material.

is calculated as the daily stock return excluding cash adjustments (such as dividends) subtracted by the daily value weighted market portfolio return excluding distributions. Data are collected for the year immediately prior and proceeding an event in order to compare to sufficient relevant days without announcements. The data are collected using the CSRP database.

Institutional ownership information for the independent variables are collected from the Thomson Reuters Financial Database (TFN, also known as CDA/Spectrum S34). The data cover institutional investors managing $100 million or more, and includes quarterly institutional investments valued over $200,000. Mutual fund data is aggregated at the parent fund level. The TFN database includes country of origin, to differentiate between foreign and domestic institutional investors. Once the institutional investors are differentiated, the percentage of firm ownership is calculated for each manager/institution. The number of large investors with at least 1% ownership of shares outstanding is then calculated for quarter immediately ended.

The analysis controls the firm size using the log of market value, collected from the CRSP dataset. In addition, industry controls are included using the Standard Industry Classification's major category codes (SIC). Other control variables included in similar studies (Larcker *et al.*, 2010), such as book value, cash and short-term investments and log sales are either statistically insignificant or economically negligible in the analyses, and are excluded. Outliers are removed by eliminating observations with a studentized residual with an absolute value greater than three.

3.4 Results

Descriptive statistics are found in Table 3.2. The average abnormal return (the one trading day holding return excluding dividends above the value

Table 3.2.   Descriptive Statistics, Panel A ($n = 1,587,084$).

Variable	Mean	Standard Deviation	Min	Max
Abnormal return	0.01	3.14	13.98	14.10
Market value ($ millions)	4,398	42,756	—	329,844
Number of large institutional investors	8.4	7.8	0	45
Number of large foreign investor funds	2.2	1.6	0	18
Number of large Asian investor funds	0.03	0.2	0	3
Percentage institutional investor	0.67	1.1	0	1
Percentage foreign	0.10	0.07	0	0.8
Percentage Asian	0.01	0.01	0	0.6

Panel B

Number of Institutional Investors with More than 1% Ownership of Shares Outstanding	Foreign Fund Frequency (%)	Asian Fund Frequency (%)
0	40.56	96.58
1	33.23	0.75
2	14.73	1.36
3	4.88	—
4	2.82	—
5	1.75	—
6	0.72	—

weighted market return) is 0.01%. It is worth noting that the average abnormal return on announcement days, at -0.13%, is significantly lower than days with no announcements, at 0.01%. This difference is significant at the $p < 0.001$ level. The market value of firms in the merged data is $4.4 billion, compared to an average market capitalization of $19 billion for the S&P500 and $13.6 billion for stocks listed on the New York Stock Exchange. The average is higher than the complete CRSP dataset average.

Firms have an average of 8.4 separate institutional investors with at least 1% ownership stake of shares outstanding. The majority of these investors (6.2 out of 8.4 on average) of these are not foreign investors; in fact, on average, there are 2.2 foreign institutional investors with a large stake. Asian investment is understandably a smaller stake, and on the vast majority of firms do not have an Asian institutional investor with a particularly large stake.

The numbers increase substantially for all types of institutional investors when looking at small (under 1% ownership) owners. Panel B underscores the distribution of significant foreign institutional investor ownership. Most of the firm-days in the sample have two large foreign institutional investor owners. Note the small frequency of large Asian investors. It is worth highlighting that a majority of firms (57%) have at least one "small" Asian institutional owner. Since the proxy proposal reform would allow investors to form groups of investors, it is plausible that Asia institutional investors could vote as a block and thus have more impact.

The analysis uses an event study concerning announcements relating to proxy access for institutional investors. A positive abnormal return above the value weighted market portfolio on an event day is assumed to capture investors' response to the news that is both unexpected and significant, i.e., the proposal announcements change the *status quo* regarding corporate governance expectations. An efficient market will react based on the expected value of proxy access to individuals firms. The hypotheses are tested for each event day, pooled event days and non-event days using the following model, following Fama *et al.* (1969):

$r_{i,t} =$ Constant

$+ \beta_1(\text{Number of Large Foreign/Asian Institutional Investors}_{i,t})$

$+ \beta_2(\text{Number of Large Domestic Institutional Investors}_{i,t})$

$+ \beta_3(\text{Log Market Value}_{i,t}) + \varepsilon_{i,t},$

where $r_{i,t}$ is the abnormal return of firm i on day t. Hypothesis 1 does not differentiate between foreign and domestic institutional investors, and uses the variables capturing the total number of large institutional investors. The hypotheses predict that the coefficients for the independent variables will be significantly different on event days than non-event days. In order to test this using the standard Fama and Macbeth (1973) methodology, separate cross-sectional regressions are run for event and non-event days for each day and the coefficients of these regressions are treated as a time series to obtain an average. These average coefficients are then tested for statistically significant differences between cross-sectional variations on non-event days compared to the specific days with announcements (Larcker *et al.*, 2010).

The tested prediction of Hypothesis 1 is that the market reaction on announcement days due to the number of large institutional investors is positive (see Table 3.3). The first column presents the baseline results for non-event days. It is interesting to note that institutional ownership has significant relationships with daily abnormal returns on days without significant system-wide proxy access events: the number of large institutional investors has a positive coefficient while the number of small institutional investors has a negative coefficient. The nature of this estimation does not lend itself to causal interpretations of these relationships, but it does underscore the need to compare event day results to an average rather than test for significance different than zero.

The second column shows the pooled results for the five announcement days. The statistics of interest is the difference between the regression results for non-event and event days, shown in the third column. There are significant and positive differences in the effect that the number of large institutional investors has on abnormal return on event days over non-event days. The difference is small — an additional large institutional investor would increase abnormal return by 0.001% extra on event days over non-event days — and the significance of the coefficient difference is largely due to the size of the non-event sample. Hypothesis 1 is supported statistically, though the economic implications appear insignificant.

Columns 4 to 8 of Table 3.3 show the results for individual announcement days. Note that for clarity, these estimations are reported as regression coefficients, rather than the difference from non-event days; coefficient differences will be discussed in the text. In line with the non-significant results

Table 3.3. Total Institutional Investor Ownership and Market Reaction.

Sample	Non-Event Days	Event Days	Event Days	14-Apr-03	30-Sep-03	24-Apr-07	26-Jul-07	19-May-09
Estimation Technique	Fama–Macbeth (1)	Fama–Macbeth (2)	Difference in Coefficients (3)	OLS (4)	OLS (5)	OLS (6)	OLS (7)	OLS (8)
Total number of large institutional investors	0.0042* (0.0018)	0.0052 (0.0186)	0.001*** (0.0000)	0.003 (0.0059)	−0.0635*** (0.0063)	0.0145* (0.0057)	0.0459*** (0.0063)	0.0260*** (0.0059)
Total number of small institutional investors	−0.0007*** (0.0001)	−0.0005 (0.0004)	0.0012*** (0.0000)	−0.0006 (0.0004)	0.0007 (0.0005)	−0.0005 (0.0004)	−0.0002 (0.0005)	−0.0017*** (0.0004)
Log market value	0.0682*** (0.0046)	0.0940** (0.0117)	0.258*** (0.0000)	0.0835** (0.0263)	0.0821** (0.0282)	0.1360*** (0.0255)	0.1003*** (0.0282)	0.0679** (0.0263)
Constant	−1.1180*** (0.1814)	−2.0446* (0.6862)	−0.927*** (0.0012)	−1.348 (2.9991)	−2.585 (3.1970)	−3.8728 (2.9027)	−2.6053 (3.2291)	0.1881 (3.0070)
Industry dummies	Y	Y		Y	Y	Y	Y	Y
R^2	0.0287	0.0288		0.0098	0.0351	0.0279	0.0493	0.0218
N	2,179,236	27,411		5,444	5,442	5,498	5,520	5,507

Note: This table shows results for Hypothesis 1. The sample contains firm-days between April 2002 and September 2004, and between April 2006 and May 2009. $+p, 0.10$; $*p < 0.05$; $**p < 0.01$; $***p < 0.001$.

Table 3.4.   Foreign and Domestic Institutional Investors and Market Reaction.

Sample	Non-Event Days	All Event Days	Non-Event Days	All Event Days
	Dependent Var: Abnormal Returns			
Estimation Technique	Fama–Macbeth (1)	Fama–Macbeth (2)	Fama–Macbeth (3)	Fama–Macbeth (4)
Number of large foreign institutional investors	−0.000106 (0.000)	0.000134*** (0.000)		
Number of large domestic institutional investors	0.0216*** (0.0010)	0.0232*** (0.000)		
Number of large Asian institutional investors			−0.0004*** (0.0000)	−0.0005*** (0.0001)
Log market value	−0.0349*** (0.0001)	−0.019*** (0.0000)	−0.000*** (0.0001)	−0.000*** (0.0001)
Constant	0.0126*** (0.0017)	0.0013*** (0.0002)	0.001*** (0.0002)	0.006*** (0.0017)
Industry dummies	Y	Y	Y	Y
R^2	0.0212	0.0002	0.0023	0.0090
N	2,064,720	27,411	1,080,141	20,033

Note: The sample contains firm-days between April 2002 and September 2004, and between April 2006 and May 2009. $+p$, 0.10; $^*p < 0.05$; $^{**}p < 0.01$; $^{***}p < 0.001$.

for the pooled announcement days' estimation, individual day results are mixed. Three of the five days show a positive and significant difference in the effect of large institutional investors compared to the non-event days (significant at $p < 0.001$).

Hypothesis 2 predicts that there will be a difference in the effect between foreign institutional investor owners and domestic institutional investors, while Hypothesis 3 predicts no effect for Asian institutional investors. Table 3.4 reports results with independent variables that break down institutional investor ownership to differentiate between country types. The first column shows the results for the Fama–Macbeth estimation for non-event days. This baseline shows that the number of large foreign institutional investor owners does not have a significant relationship with abnormal returns, while large domestic institutional investors have a positive, economically insignificant relationship. Repeating the model for the pooled announcement days in Column 2 shows a similar insignificant relationship. Hypothesis 2 is thus rejected, and the empirical evidence supports the view that firms with large foreign institutional investors are not positively or adversely affected when the probability of proxy access increases.

Columns 3 and 4 repeat this process for Asian institutional investors (though without the interest in the marginal effect over domestic investors). Column 3 shows the results for the Fama–Macbeth estimation for non-event days for large Asian investors. Like the broader foreign investor results discussed above, the baseline shows that the number of large Asian institutional investors does not have an economically significant relationship with abnormal returns. On event days, shown in Column 4, the relationship is not changed.

3.5 Discussion and Conclusion

Proxy access could increase the influence of institutional investors, including foreign owners. This study examines this issue, with a particular focus on Asian institutional investors. While a number of studies have investigated the behavior of large institutional investors, and the relationship between ownership and firm behavior, this analysis measures market reaction based on institutional investor composition to events that significantly raise the possibility of increased shareholder power. In addition, the study is able to deal with the significant issue of ownership endogeneity by using exogenous proxy access policy announcement events for variation; this issue is a frequent problem in estimation when dealing with institutional investor ownership and other firm characteristics.

The results of this study suggest that Asian institutional investors do not have an impact on firm value, at least in the immediate aftermath of news that increases the probability of monitoring. This mirrors the broader results for foreign institutional investors, in contrast to the baseline result that large (mostly domestic) owners do have an impact on proxy proposal event days.

There are limitations to the study that could threaten the identification and create spurious results. Many of the largest foreign institutional investors are not included in the data, either due to their investment strategies or because of the screening procedures. In addition, the study does not differentiate between the multiple types of institutional investors, such as sovereign wealth funds, hedge funds, private equity and mutual funds.

It is clear that in many cases, corporate boards did not fulfill their mission to monitor management on behalf of the shareholders. The nature of the crises, however, highlights that firms require directors with specialized knowledge and board members with special interests may actually be detrimental. There is agreement that understanding the effects of proxy access is necessary as we consider future policies. In an era of globalization and agency capitalism, as so much of corporate governance in practice is in the hands of institutional investors, policy makers will need to fully consider the many variations and motivations within this group.

References

Admati, AR, P Pfleiderer and J Zechner (1994). Large shareholder activism, risk sharing, and financial market equilibrium. *J. Polit. Econ.*, 102, 1097–1130.

Almazan, A, JC Hartzell and LT Starks (2005). Active institutional shareholders and costs of monitoring: Evidence from executive compensation. *Financial Manag.*, 34, 5–34.

Aronson, B (2005). What can we learn from US corporate governance? A critical analysis. *J. Law Pol.*, 2.

Bebchuk, LA (2003). The case for shareholder access to the ballot. *Bus. Law.*, 59, 43.

Bebchuk, LA (2007). The myth of the shareholder franchise. *Virginia Law Review*, 93, 675–732.

Black, BS (1992). Institutional investors and corporate governance: The case for institutional voice. *J. Appl. Corp. Finance*, 5, 19–32.

Campbell, JY, AW Lo, AC MacKinlay and RF Whitelaw (1997). *The Econometrics of Financial Markets*. Princeton: University Press Princeton.

Chandler, WBC (1999). On the instructiveness of insiders, independents, and institutional investors. *U. Cin. L. Rev.*, 67, 1083–1090.

Chhibber, PK and SK Majumdar (1999). Foreign ownership and profitability: Property rights, control, and the performance of firms in Indian industry. *J. Law Econ.*, 42, 209–238.

Dahlquist, M and G Robertsson (2001). Direct foreign ownership, institutional investors, and firm characteristics. *Journal of Financial Economics*, 59(3), 413–440.

David, P, M Bloom and AJ Hillman (2007). Investor activism, managerial responsiveness, and corporate social performance. *Strateg. Manag. J.*, 28(1), 91–100.

Del Guercio, D and J Hawkins (1999). The motivation and impact of pension fund activism. *J. Financial Econ.*, 52, 293–340.

Demsetz, H and K Lehn (1985). The structure of corporate ownership: Causes and consequences. *J. Polit. Econ.*, 93.

Demsetz, H and B Villalonga (2001). Ownership structure and corporate performance. *J. Corp. Finance*, 7, 209–233.

Dimelis, S and H Louri (2002). Foreign ownership and production efficiency: A quantile regression analysis. *Oxf. Econ. Pap.*, 54, 449.

Fama, E, L Fisher, M Jensen and R Roll (1969). The adjustment of stock prices to new information. *International Economic Review*, 10.

Fama, EF and J MacBeth (1973). Risk, return and equilibrium: Some empirical tests. *J. Polit. Econ.*, 81, 607–636.

Gillan, S and LT Starks (2007). The evolution of shareholder activism in the United States. *J. Appl. Corp. Finance*, 19, 55–73.

Gillan, S and L Starks (2003). Corporate governance, corporate ownership, and the role of institutional investors: A global perspective. *Weinberg Center for Corporate Governance Working Paper*, (2003–01).

Gillan, SL and LT Starks (2000). Corporate governance proposals and shareholder activism: The role of institutional investors. *Journal of Financial Economics*, 57(2), 275–305.

Gilson, RJ (2007). Leo strine's third way: Responding to agency capitalism. *J. Corp. L.*, 33, 47.

Gordon, JN (2008). Proxy contests in an era of increasing shareholder power: Forget issuer proxy access and focus on e-proxy. *Vand. L. Rev.*, 61, 475.

GPFG (2009). Norway government pension fund global annual report 2009. Ministry of Finance.

Han, S (2003). National pension fund management in Korea. Presented at World Bank Conference on Public Pension Fund Management, 5–7 May 2003.

Hansen, GS and CWL Hill (1991). Are institutional investors myopic? A time-series study of four technology-driven industries. *Strateg. Manag. J.*, 12, 1–16.

Hotchkiss, ES and D Strickland (2003). Does shareholder composition matter? Evidence from the market reaction to corporate earnings announcements. *J. Finance*, 58, 1469–1498.

Jackson, J (2008). Foreign ownership of U.S. financial assets: Implications of a withdrawal. CRS Report for Congress, 14 January.

Jensen, MC and WH Meckling (1976). Theory of the firm: Managerial behavior, agency costs and ownership structure. *J. Financial Econ.*, 3, 305–360.

Johnson, RA and DW Greening (1999). The effects of corporate governance and institutional ownership types on corporate social performance. *Acad. Manag. J.*, 42, 564–576.

Kotter, J and U Lel (2008). Friends or foes? The stock price impact of sovereign wealth fund investments and the price of keeping secrets. *Int. Finance Discussion Pap.*, 940.

Larcker, D, G Ormazabal and D Taylor (2010). The regulation of corporate governance. *Stanford University Corporate Governance Research Program* Working Paper, 18 January.

Larcker, DF, G Ormazabal and DJ Taylor (2011). The market reaction to corporate governance regulation. *Journal of Financial Economics*, 101(2), 431–448.

Listokin, S (2011). Public pension fund activism: A review of the largest government pension systems. *IUP J. Governance Pub. Policy*, 4, 35–49.

Listokin, S (2012). Proxy access and ownership: Does institutional investor type matter. *Int. J. Corporate Governance*, 2, 288–304.

McConnell, JJ and H Servaes (1990). Additional evidence on equity ownership and corporate value. *J. Financial Econ.*, 27, 595–612.

Neubaum, DO and SA Zahra (2006). Institutional ownership and corporate social performance: The moderating effects of investment horizon, activism, and coordination. *Journal of Management*, 32(1), 108–131.

Pollock, AJ (2007). Will the real shareholders please stand up? Principals and agents in the Sarbanes–Oxley era. *Financial Services Outlook*, 19 July.

Pozen, RC (2003). Institutional perspective on shareholder nominations of corporate directors. *Bus. Law*, 59, 95.

Qui, L (2003). Public pension fund activism and M&A activity. Yale School of Management, International Center of Finance.

Romano, R (1993). Public pension fund activism in corporate governance reconsidered. *Colum. L. Rev.*, 93, 795.

Romano, R (2003). Does confidential proxy voting matter? *Journal of Legal Studies*, 32, 465–509.

SEC (2009). Facilitating shareholder director nominations release nos. 33-9046. Securities and Exchange Commission.

Shleifer, A and RW Vishny (1986). Large shareholders and corporate control. *J. Polit. Econ.*, 94.

Smith, MP (1996). Shareholder activism by institutional investors: Evidence from CalPERS. *J. Finance*, 51, 227–252.

Steverman, B and D Bogoslaw (2008). The financial crisis blame game. *Bus. Week*, 10 December.

Strine Jr, LE (2007). Toward common sense and common ground-reflections on the shared interests of managers and labor in a more rational system of corporate governance. *J. Corp. L.*, 33, 1.

Wahal, S (2009). Pension fund activism and firm performance. *J. Financial Quant. Analysis*, 31, 1–23.

Woidtke, T (2002). Agents watching agents?: Evidence from pension fund ownership and firm value. *J. Financial Econ.*, 63, 99–131.

Part II

Integration and Investment

Chapter 4

Post-Foreign Entry Decisions by Global Retailers in Asian and non-Asian Markets: Like or Unlike?

Sonia Ketkar[1]

4.1 Introduction

An article (2006) titled, *"Emerging Market Priorities for Global Retailers"* provided by the consulting firm, A. T. Kearney that publishes the Global Retail Development Index stated that with respect to emerging markets, "countries must create the right competitive environment to attract foreign companies and thereby reap the economic benefits that increased retail activity can provide". The direct foreign investment and international business literatures tend to converge on the conviction in this regard that lowered political and economic risk creates such an environment and encourages investment by multinational firms. Nations should thus invest in governance infrastructure, improvements so that FDI inflows can increase (Globerman and Shapiro, 2002). From a foreign or host government's perspective, it is important that multinational firms that have entered the market continue to increase their investments. But do they indeed increase investment as governance structures improve? I examine this research question in this study.

The recent decades have witnessed rapid internationalization by firms into emerging nations as countries have increasingly reduced their barriers to trade and investment. Global retailers have also responded to these

[1]I would like to thank Ramkishen Rajan, Zoltan Acs, Siona Listokin, the participants of the research workshop on Globalization, Growth and Governance held at the Institute of Southeast Asian Studies, Singapore and the attendees at the brown bag series at the School of Public Policy, George Mason University for their comments and suggestions.

new opportunities in such markets that are also characterized by a growing consuming population and in many cases weak domestic competitors (Bianchi and Ostale, 2006). This trend has been particularly marked in Asia which boasts of contributing 32% of global retail sales for firms (Kearney, 2006) and consists of untapped regions with high potential for growth. Due to these reasons, South East Asian markets in particular have been much sought after by global retailers.

In the years around the Asian Financial Crisis (1997), many global retailers started internationalizing quickly as the industry diversified geographically outside of North America and Western Europe. Many of these firms entered Asia, especially the South East which was liberalizing and privatizing at record speed around this time.

In some ways, the economic crisis in these countries created conditions for entry for these firms for the following reasons. The International Monetary Fund (IMF) stepped in to bail out the nations in crisis, mainly Thailand, South Korea and Indonesia, although their neighbors such as Singapore, Hong Kong, Malaysia and others were also seriously affected by the financial turmoil. In addition to taking into account recommendations by the IMF to keep their markets open to foreigners and allow foreign firms to own larger percentages in domestic operations, the currencies of these countries lost significant value thus creating additional incentives to be prime acquisition targets. Several global retailers such as France's Carrefour and United States' Wal-Mart entered South Korea and Belgium-based Etablissements Delhaize got a footing in Thailand around the year 1997.

Later on, well-known economist Paul Krugman (1998) called such purchases of domestic firms by global firms around the time of the crisis as "fire-sales". He argued that in reality, it was local firms that are the most efficient "owners" of some firms but due to their lower prices, foreign firms were able to buy them out. Foreign firms were actually inefficient owners of the acquired companies. Then, there were no data available to confirm or refute his ideas. Some might argue that we still do not have strong or sufficient data and that is probably a true statement. There are many other internal, firm-related as well as environmental factors that affect cross-border acquisitions along with their success or failure which makes it hard to draw conclusions.

One approach to determine whether foreign firms are indeed better owners of retail firms in emerging Asia would be to examine their post-foreign entry decisions. Foreign direct investment has an inherent long-term component in that firms that enter foreign markets by way of subsidiaries expect to pursue expansion opportunities as they come along. Although many firms do not survive in foreign markets, survival and profitability are priority goals (Chung and Beamish, 2005; Li, 1995). Therefore, *as governance infrastructure improves in emerging economies, the expectation is that firms will be more likely to increase their investments in those regions.* Increased regulatory quality and government effectiveness would reduce the risk and uncertainty in that market thereby creating incentives for increased investment subject to firm ability, willingness and financial capability. I use Globerman and Shapiro's conceptualization of governance infrastructure which "comprises public institutions and policies created by governments as a framework for economic and social relations" (Globerman and Shapiro, 2002, p. 1901).

The international business field is replete with studies that have investigated the firm-specific factors that influence firm entry decisions but issues related to governance infrastructure have been largely ignored. Research in the policy field has focused primarily on governance, I bring these fields together loosely to explore the post-foreign entry investment and divestment actions of global retail firms (the reason for this choice of industry is explained later on in the chapter). The level of analysis is the firm's investment decision in the host market. With the aim of focusing on the developing Asian markets that are constantly in the current news for being the fastest growing regions in the world, I compare these activities of retailers in Asian and non-Asian markets. The purpose of the comparison is to determine whether there are differences in firm investment behavior in Asia. If so, clearly there is a need to probe these differences further. If not, it is possible to contemplate (although certainly not confirm) that foreign firms might be efficient owners of assets in Asia or that at least in the global retail industry, the decisions to invest in Asia were not necessarily driven by the lower asset prices but also by internal firm factors that were somewhat independent of the time period of the crisis.

The nature of this study is also influenced by the characteristics of the sample selected. Although details about the sample and methodology are provided later on in the chapter, at this point it is important to note that in the case of the data that pertain to firms in Asia, 95% of those firms entered the Asian markets in the time period starting from 1996. Hence, they form a suitable sample to examine the ownership issue.

The remainder of the chapter is organized in this manner. Following this introduction, I briefly refer to the theoretical underpinnings of the study. The next section discusses the context of the global retail industry. That discussion is followed by a description of the data, method and results and includes a comparison of global (including Asia) and non-Asian datasets. The final section centers on examining and explaining the findings and conclusions.

4.2 Theoretical Overview

As mentioned earlier, there is a fundamental belief in the foreign direct investment (FDI) literature that FDI promotes growth and efficiency in host countries. But, in order to maximize its benefits, the regulatory framework should be "supportive" of FDI. Many emerging country governments have put incentives in place to bring in foreign firms. More importantly, once foreign firms are present in the economy, they face liabilities of foreignness (Kostova and Zaheer, 1999; Zaheer, 1995) or the increased costs of doing business in an institutionally different environment (Scott, 1995).

Research has shown that government investments in bettering their policies and the enforcement of those policies can create an improved environment for foreign firms to enter and do business. Similarly, such improvements are also an impetus for the growth of domestic firms. There can be two possible outcomes to increasing the efficiency and effectiveness of the regulatory system in host countries. The first is which foreign firms that have entered the market are able to overcome the liabilities of foreignness alluded to above. This is especially true in the case of firms whose home countries belong to the industrialized world. In their case, evolving governance in host markets would initiate the development of regulatory structures in their foreign market that grants a sense of trust in the government that is similar to that perceived or experienced in their home countries. Furthermore, this perception of lowered risk and uncertainty related to the government creates conditions suitable for additional investment in that market if the financial resources are available to the firm. Hence,

*H*1: A one-unit improvement (increase) in governance infrastructure in the host market post-foreign entry would lead firms to increase investment.

There are some authors who draw conclusions that are contrary to the above arguments about improved governance. Most of these have been with respect to environmental policy because increased regulation would serve to deter FDI (Globerman and Shapiro, 2002). An article on the Russian retail sector published by PlanetRetail (2010) brought out how the introduction and implementation of a law that would make pricing more transparent and competition less monopolistic would actually encourage increases in prices of some products and possibly corruption. We can expect that global retailers operating in Russia will find it hard to manage some of the fall out of the law, although the existence and enforcement of policy in this case should in fact lower the risk for such firms. Firms might respond to such changes by decreasing investment in their existing operation with the intention of sharing ownership with a local company in order to "learn" or then with the potential option to exit the country completely later on (Benito and Gripsrud, 1992).

The argument might also hold weight if the main reason due to which a firm entered a particular foreign country was to take advantage of a weakness in the system at a point in time such as during the Asian Financial Crisis when Asian firms were cheaper to buy out. In such cases, improved governance might actually create additional costs and risks to operating in that market. Therefore, one could also suggest that:

*H*2: A one-unit improvement (increase) in governance infrastructure in the host market post-foreign entry would lead firms to decrease investment.

It is necessary to note that other firms or environmental factors can exist that act as moderators or mediators in these investment decisions. But since the goal is to isolate the association between improving governance infrastructure and investment or divestment (decreased investment) decisions post-foreign entry, those other factors are outside the scope of the study and hence not discussed here. In the next section, I discuss the nature of the global retail industry.

4.3 The Global Retail Industry

The global retail industry is dominated by a few large firms that are fairly aggressive in their foreign expansion efforts mainly entering new foreign markets through horizontal acquisitions of domestic or international competitors' retail chains. In the 1990s, global retailers rapidly entered developing economies, attracted by the growing consumer base and their increasing purchasing power. While most of these firms have been immensely successful in their home markets, they have been relatively unsuccessful in transferring their competitive advantages to host markets (Bianchi and Ostale, 2006). Similar to entry mode, expansion in host markets also often takes the form of acquisitions.

All these firms originated in the developed economies and spent the years prior to the mid-1990s expanding into their neighbors for the most part, but from then on have increasingly turned their attention to the developing regions in Asia, South America and Eastern Europe. In a bid to outdo their global industry rivals, these firms have often expanded aggressively through acquisitions of existing local operators which gives them an overnight presence in the host market. The failure rate in this industry has been very high. For example, France's Carrefour entered and exited around six to seven foreign markets in a 10-year period, the latest being Russia. Some of these, they hope to re-enter in the future.

The leading firms have often turned countries into battle grounds as they compete for market leadership. For example, Wal-Mart is planning to grow organically in Mexico ever since Carrefour exited the market in 2005. The largest retailer has also held back on plans to enter Colombia due to the presence of Carrefour and Casino (Moreau, 2009). Global retailers such as Wal-Mart and Carrefour have bought out national or domestic operators and hence grown larger. There is a missing link in the existing literature in terms of understanding the post-internationalization behavior of global retailers (Bianchi and Ostale, 2006). I attempt to shed light on this matter by focusing on this industry. Furthermore, corporate research has proved time and again that cross-sectional studies are unable to reveal unique industry trends or patterns. Holding the industry as a constant serves to address that point and better improve our knowledge on a specific area.

Global retailers carry horizontal FDI in that they are market seekers, produce output in different locations and as a result need to re-establish their supply chain in individual foreign markets or regions close to those markets in order to operate efficiently. Thus, economies of scale are low but sunk costs are high as are the costs of entry and exit.

Some might argue that the global retail industry should strategize to be locally responsive in host markets because of the culture-specific nature of retail services. Therefore, operating in a foreign country can be challenging on various accounts. Difficulty in operating in culturally distant markets can be exacerbated by the weaker governance infrastructure in those nations. Thus, the context of the global retail industry provides a suitable milieu in which to examine the issues identified in the previous section.

4.4 Methodology

4.4.1 *Sample*

The sample of global retailers contained data on foreign entries, increased investments and decreased investments (including some exits) by these firms in the period from 1996 to 2008. This time period was selected for a number of reasons. First, barring a few foreign investments in geographically bordering countries, most retailers started expanding rapidly in the 1990s due to globalization and lowering of borders. Second, I accessed data on the institutional factors from the World Governance Indicators database that is published from 1996 onward which broadly matched the timing of internationalization activities of the retail firms.

The unit of analysis was the firm decision related to entry, increased investment or decreased investment. To create the sample, I identified the sample of firms whose decisions were examined by way of standard industrial classification (SIC) and North American industry classification system (NAICS) codes for the global retail industry. I included those firms that had operations in at least five foreign markets in order to control for the effect of newness and invariably focused on retailers that were comparatively experienced in foreign operations because newly internationalized firms go through different challenges that might confound the results. I conducted multiple searches on the retail firms on popular databases such as Hoovers, Mergent, Lexis–Nexis and others and examined these firms' history and other activities to identify their decisions. Where possible, I matched information from different data sources for confirmation.

Since the overall goal was to compare investments by global retailers in Asia as opposed to that in non-Asian countries, I created and tested two datasets, one including decisions made by firms in Asian countries and the second without the Asian part in the sample. The description of the datasets is as below.

In the first dataset including Asia, the total number of these firms' foreign decisions in 44 host markets was 169; 69 foreign entries, 53 increased investments, 15 decreased investments, 11 later exits and 21 early exits (less one due to missing data). The eight global retailers hailed from seven different home countries namely the United States, the United Kingdom, Germany, France, Belgium and the Netherlands, all developed countries. The second dataset sans investments in Asia included 130 decisions; 47 entries, 45 increased investments and 38 decreased investments.

4.4.2 Variables[2]

4.4.2.1 Governance infrastructure (host context)

This construct was measured based on the host country's score on government effectiveness, political stability, regulatory quality, rule of law and corruption in the year of the event. These values were obtained from the World Governance Indicators database developed by the World Bank. This dataset has been popularly employed in many academic studies. Due to the high correlation between these five dimensions and therefore the possibility of multicollinearity, I added them to give the host nation a total score in that year and then took an average value for the variable. The total score in that year respectively became the host context score which reflects the construct of governance infrastructure of that country in that year.

4.4.2.2 Event

This construct took on a value of one for firm entry into the foreign country, two for increased investment and three for divestment. This tri-level variable was the dependent indicator in the model.

---

[2]Same nomenclature used in both datasets.

4.4.2.3 *Control variables*

Firms are known to make investment decisions based on economic indicators for host markets such as gross domestic product (GDP) level and/or GDP growth per capita, which is also an indicator of growth in market size. Specifically in the case of the retail industry, firm decisions might also be based on increase in household spending. Therefore, I included these as control variables in the models. However, I found that household income and GDP level had no significant effect on firm activities in foreign markets. Therefore, those results are not included here. However, GDP annual growth per capita did influence firm decisions and it was included in the models. Those results are shown in the following sections.

4.4.3 *Analysis*

I performed multinomial logit regression in many stages. This statistical method is very robust and thus provides sufficient confidence in the findings. I first ran exploratory models using the control variables. Since the samples included incumbent firms, I regressed the variable, governance infrastructure (host context) on the tri-level dependent variable using foreign entry as the base level. That permitted me to compare subsequent decisions of increased or decreased investment as they vary with improving governance and as compared to that during foreign entry into that host nation. The same analyses were performed in the exact same sequence on both datasets (including Asia and sans Asia). The results are as presented in Sec. 4.5.

4.5 Results

4.5.1 *Models including global retailers in Asia*

The overall model was significant ($p < 0.01$) with a pseudo R-square of 10%. The results are included in Table 4.1. As compared with foreign entry, a one-unit increase (improvement) in governance infrastructure does not significantly influence firm's decisions to increase investment in the host market. However, the improvement is associated with a decrease in investment ($p < 0.001$). The significant but negative coefficient ($B = -1.266$, $p < 0.001$) for the interaction term between governance and GDP growth per capita indicates that as compared with

Table 4.1.   Results for Model Including Investments in Asia.

Event Base Level: Entries	Variable	Coefficient	Standard Error	Significance
Increased investment	Intercept	−0.047	0.264	0.859
	governance infrastructure (Gov)	0.978	0.613	0.110
	Gov * GDP per cap	−0.663	0.390	0.089
Decreased investment	Intercept	−0.389	0.297	0.190
	governance infrastructure (Gov)	2.026	0.615	0.001
	Gov * GDP per cap	−1.266	0.396	0.001

Table 4.2.   Results for Model Sans Investments in Asia.

Event Base Level: Entries	Variable	Coefficient	Standard Error	Significance
Increased investment	Intercept	0.567	0.367	0.123
	governance infrastructure (Gov)	0.868	0.718	0.227
	Gov * GDP per cap	−0.778	0.445	0.081
Decreased investment	Intercept	0.110	0.414	0.792
	governance infrastructure (Gov)	1.925	0.729	0.008
	Gov * GDP per cap	−1.330	0.453	0.003

foreign entry, an improvement in governance infrastructure is associated with decreased investments by firms but that relationship changes if GDP per capita is also increasing, in which case firms would in fact be less likely to decrease their investment. This model also supports Hypothesis 2.

4.5.2 *Model sans global retailers in Asia*

The overall model was significant ($p < 0.01$) with a pseudo R-square of 13%. These results are included in Table 4.2. As compared with foreign entry, a one-unit increase (improvement) in governance infrastructure does not significantly influence firm decisions to increase investment in the host market. However, the improvement is associated with a decrease in investment ($p < 0.01$). The significant but negative coefficient ($B = -1.330$, $p < 0.01$) for the interaction term between governance and GDP growth per capita indicates that as compared with foreign entry, an improvement in governance infrastructure is associated with decreased investments by firms but that relationship changes if GDP per capita is also increasing, in which case firms would in fact be less likely to decrease their investment. This model also supports Hypothesis 2 and the overall results are similar to Model 1 which includes investments in all countries including Asia.

4.5.3 *Post-hoc tests for Asian sample*

I further examined the sample of 38 firms' decisions in Asia only in an exploratory manner. As seen in Fig. 4.1, the governance infrastructure was stronger during foreign entry and firms seemed to increase their investments even as it weakened in the years following entry. However, at the time that firms made decisions to decrease their investment, the governance

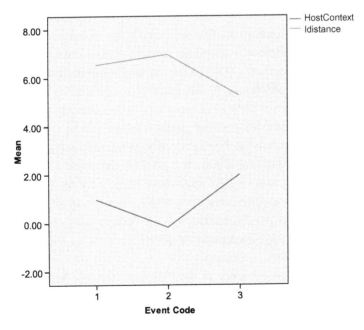

Fig. 4.1. Asian Sample.

had actually improved. The appendix includes charts which show changing trends year-on-year (from 1996 to 2008) for the different indicators of governance for the South East Asian countries. The discussion related to these findings is in the next section.

4.6 Discussion and Conclusion

The general consensus in the political economy and international business literatures remains that a stable and predictable regulatory environment attracts a higher level of FDI into a host nation (Rivoli and Solario, 1996). While that might be true in many cases, it is not a universal trend. As illustrated in this study, in the case of global retailer firms that internationalized rapidly in the years following 1996, positive changes in governance infrastructure in host countries did not necessarily lead to increased investments as compared with entry decisions. Instead, such changes were associated with decreased investments by global retail firms. Although somewhat unexpected, there could be multiple reasons for these findings.

The mid-1990s onward saw many erstwhile protectionist countries undertaking policy reforms (Roland, 2001). This gave rise to an even greater number of multinational firms that were ready to take advantage of this bigger global marketplace. According to the United Nations Conference on Trade and Development (UNCTAD), the number of multinational firms increased from approximately 40,000 in 1995 to over 82,000 in 2010. This time period also appears to have coincided with the saturation of domestic markets in developed countries for global retailers and the maturation of the industry which enhanced their motivation to internationalize quickly as competitors followed the same path. It is possible that some of these entries often to culturally distant regions might have been hasty decisions brought on by all of the above conditions. As a result, some years later when they could not perform as per expectations in the foreign markets, some firms decided to decrease their investment or quit those markets, evolving governance notwithstanding.

There is also some evidence in the FDI literature that bettering governance infrastructure not only promotes foreign investment but also lends itself to the growth of domestic industry. A good example is the Indian retail sector which has historically been protected from foreign competition and until 2013 was closed to multi-brand although not single brand foreign retailers. While foreign firms enter, the domestic retail industry has started flourishing with easier access to capital. Domestic firms, especially those in location-specific industries such as some types of retail operations (e.g., grocery stores), enjoy the benefits of having intimate knowledge of the cultural requirements of consumers while foreigners struggle to gain the same information at a cost. Hence, improving governance increases domestic competition to foreign firms and in some industries that need to be locally responsive, might serve to deter increases in investment by foreign firms.

As one of the goals of the study was to observe firm activities of investment in Asian economies, the findings indicate that firms did not behave differently in Asia. A comparison of the global dataset including retailer decisions in Asia to the database excluding Asian investments did not show any differences. This shows that, although the Asian economies witnessed an increase in inward FDI in the aftermath of the Asian Financial Crisis, they also saw decreased investments by global retailers. Without additional information and data, it is difficult and presumptuous to determine that the findings of this study provide sufficient evidence for fire sales because the exact same results were achieved upon analysis of the dataset excluding Asian investments. If the global retailers had indeed taken advantage of the attractively valued Asian firms at the time, we might have seen a different pattern emerge with the different datasets.

The significance and direction of the interaction effect between improved governance and GDP per capita is interesting, albeit in keeping with existing knowledge about FDI. I found that in the case of both datasets and models, positively evolving governance infrastructure was related to the likelihood of decreased investments by firms. However, in the presence of increasing GDP per capita, this probability changed such that it reduced the likelihood that firms would decrease their investments. We can surmise that in spite of pressures to divest, firms might hold onto their investments when the overall consumer income is moving upward with the expectation that they can improve performance or increase investment and the like in the future. Equally interesting was the early discovery that GDP level is not associated with investment decisions although FDI studies have frequently supported this view (Globerman and Shapiro, 2002). Whereas GDP, which can be a proxy for the economic potential of a country, is an important antecedent of foreign entry decisions, it is not a major factor in subsequent investment or divestment decisions after foreign entry.

There was an exploratory element to the analysis for the 38 decisions by global retailers in Asia. Since the sample size by itself is too small to perform statistical analysis, I developed charts which exposed trends in the data. Figure 4.1 plots the three decisions on the x-axis (1 = entry, 2 = increased investment, 3 = decreased investments) and the y-axis plots mean values. The trends' line in the bottom half of the graph supports the overall findings in the larger samples. I also included another dimension to the graph which is represented by the line titled "distance" in the upper half of the picture. This line captures the difference in the governance infrastructure as measured by its five sub-components taken together (regulatory quality, rule of law, corruption, government effectiveness and political stability) between the retailer's home country and host Asian country. The diagram indicates that during decreased investment or divestment decisions, there were fewer differences, i.e., more similar governance structures in both home and host markets. This finding might seem counter-intuitive to the internationalization literature popularized by Johanson and Vahlne (1977) and supported almost unanimously by other international business studies that examined globalization behavior of multinational firms. However, again, the patterns are similar to the overall findings and hence the reasoning above applies here as well.

This study has managerial and theoretical implications. Theoretically, the conclusion that firms might in some cases decrease investments while governance infrastructure is improving contradicts the basis of foreign direct investment studies although as pointed out, there are reasonable explanations for it. As for the managerial aspect, we have seen several instances in which firms have made hasty foreign entry decisions. These can be especially risky in culturally and institutionally distant markets (Barkema _et al._, 1996; Kogut and Singh, 1988). In some cases, these decisions are a response to government incentives or other attractive opportunities such as the possibility of fire sales. At other times, it might be the urgency to follow a rival to a particular region or gain first mover advantage in another market in order to pre-empt a competitor. Regardless, due to the high sunk costs involved in FDI decisions, it is important for managers to rationalize their decisions and avoid some of the pitfalls identified here.

There are also some limitations to this study. First and foremost, I have attempted to maintain a tone of "association" or "relationship" between the constructs used in the study rather than causality which is often very difficult to establish. Furthermore, there are various firm factors that impact the decision to increase or decrease investment in foreign operations and these, although crucial, have not been taken into consideration in this study. They are and have been the bailiwick of several other studies and leaving them out helped me broadly isolate the link with governance factors. Finally, the results shown here pertain to one industry only — the global retail industry. Therefore, it is not possible to suggest any generalizability unless other firms and decisions from other industries are also included. Additionally, all the firms which made the investment decisions belong to industrialized home countries and majority of their decisions were made in developing host countries. Therefore, the decisions might take on a different nature if those conditions are altered.

In conclusion, based on this study, post-foreign entry decisions by global retailers in Asian and non-Asian markets are — like!

References

Barkema, H, J Bell and J Pennings (1996). Foreign entry, cultural barriers and learning. *Strateg. Manag. J.*, 17, 151–166.

Benito, GRG and G Gripsrud (1992). The expansion of foreign direct investments: Discrete rational location choices or a cultural learning process? *J. Int. Bus. Stud.*, 23, 461–476.

Bianchi, C and E Ostale (2006). Lessons learned from unsuccessful internationalization attempts: Examples of multinational retailers in Chile. *J. Bus. Res.*, 59, 140–147.

Chung, C and P Beamish (2005). The impact of institutional reforms on character-istics and survival of foreign subsidiaries in emerging economies. *J. Manag. Stud.*, 42, 35–62.

Globerman, S and D Shapiro (2002). Global foreign direct investment flows: The role of governance infrastructure. *World Dev.*, 30, 1899–1919.

Johanson, J and J Vahlne (1977). The internationalization process of the firm — A model of knowledge development and increasing foreign market commit-ments. *J. Int. Bus. Stud.*, 8, 23–32.

Kearney, AT (2006). Emerging market priorities for global retailers. *The Global Retail Development Index.*

Kogut, B and H Singh (1988). The effect of national culture on the choice of entry mode. *J. Int. Bus. Stud.*, 19, 411–432.

Kostova, T and S Zaheer (1999). Organizational legitimacy under conditions of complexity: The case of the multinational enterprise. *Academy Manag. Rev.*, 24, 64–81.

Krugman, P (1998). Fire-sale FDI. NBER Conference on capital flows to emerging markets, 20–21 February.

Li, J (1995). Foreign entry and survival: Effects of strategic choices on performance in international markets. *Strateg. Manag. J.*, 16, 333–351.

Moreau, R (2009). Carrefour, casino and Wal-Mart's expansion strategies in Latin America. *Retail Dig.*, 22 June.

PlanetRetail (2010). How will new government regulations impact the Russian retail? Milos Ryba, PlanetRetail Insight 8–9.

Rivoli, P and E Solario (1996). Foreign direct investment and investment under uncertainty. *J. Int. Bus. Stud.*, 27, 335–357.

Roland, G (2001). Ten years after: Transition and economics. *IMF Staff Papers*: *Transition economies: How much progress?* 48, 29–52.

Scott, R (1995). *Institutions and Organizations.* Thousand Oaks, CA: Sage.

Zaheer, S (1995). Overcoming the liability of foreignness. *Academy Manag. J.*, 38, 341–363.

Appendix 1

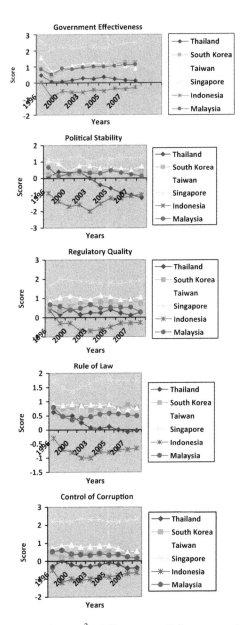

Fig. A1 Changes in the Indicators[3] of Governance Infrastructure in South East Asian Countries From 1996 to 2008.

---

[3]Figures are developed based on data from World Development Indicators.

Chapter 5

Intra-ASEAN FDI Flows and the Role of China and India: Trends and Determinants

Rabin Hattari, Ramkishen S. Rajan and Shandre Thangavelu

5.1 Introduction

The phenomenon of south–south foreign direct investment (FDI) flows, particularly those arising from China and India, has generated significant interest among policymakers, academia and the popular press in recent times. Available data from the World Bank indicates south–south FDI to have increased almost three-fold (from US$14 billion in 1995 to US$47 billion in 2003), and accounts for almost 37% of total FDI flows to developing countries, up from 15% in 1995 (see Table 5.1). The Association of South East Asian Nations (ASEAN) grouping is not an exception to this phenomenon. FDI from ASEAN economies has expanded rapidly beyond its borders, especially intra-regionally (Hiratsuka, 2006).

Intra-ASEAN FDI flows can be traced back to the 1997 East Asian financial crisis which caused a severe region-wide recession. The crisis also adversely affected output, currencies, stock markets, other asset prices and capital inflows across ASEAN member countries. ASEAN members experienced a drastic decline of about US$12 billion in the net FDI flows from 1997 to 1998. Table 5.2 shows the relative shares of global and Asian FDI inflows and outflows. As it is apparent, developing Asia dominates both as sources and destinations of FDI in terms of both stocks and flows among the developing countries. It is interesting to note that during the period after crisis (from 1998 to 2000), the average ASEAN share of FDI inflows declined to a low of 2.3% compared to a high 5% on average between 1988

Table 5.1.   Growing Importance of South–South FDI, 1995–2003 (US$ billions).

	1995	1999	2000	2001	2002	2003
Total inflows (1)	90.3	163.5	154.7	159.3	135.3	129.6
From high-income OECD (2)	48.1	95.4	93.7	84.8	55.1	59.4
From high-income non-OECD (3)	28.2	35.0	22.7	24.8	27.2	22.8
South–South FDI (1) − (2) − (3)	14.0	33.1	38.3	49.7	53.0	47.4
South–South FDI (percent)	15.5	20.2	24.8	31.2	39.2	36.6

Source: World Bank (2006).
Notes: The south–south estimates are based on 35 countries that account for 85% of the total FDI flows to developing countries. The estimates are based on the World Bank's classification of developing countries.

and 1990, while their FDI outflows increased. During this period, the role of China in the world economy has exponentially increased. About 40% of total FDI inflows to the Asian region have been directed to China. Many view that China's large domestic market and low labor cost are attracting more FDI to the country. While India is a relatively late-comer and its industrialization strategy is much less dependent on FDI, its vast pool of skilled workers, strong institutional quality, and large domestic market has begun to attract greater global and regional FDI inflows. Both China and India are also significant exporters of capital, including FDI.

This chapter uses bilateral FDI flows data to investigate FDI trends, and the role of macroeconomic, financial and institutional variables in facilitating intra-ASEAN FDI flows over the period 1990–2004. This chapter will also examine the extent and determinants of FDI flows between ASEAN, China and India. Eichengreen and Tong (2007), Liu *et al.* (2007) and Sudsawasd and Chaisrisawatsuk (2006) are three of possibly just a handful of papers that examine FDI to Asia using bilateral data. However, these papers only consider FDI from OECD economies as the source country since they use data from the OECD.[1] In contrast, the focus of this chapter is on selected ASEAN economies, India, and China as the sources of FDI

---

[1]A selective list of recent papers that use bilateral FDI data from OECD but are not specifically limited to Asia are Bénassy-Quéré *et al.* (2007), Head and Ries (2008), Lougani *et al.* (2002). Razin *et al.* (2003), Razin *et al.* (2005) and Stein and Daude (2007).

Table 5.2.   Distribution of FDI by Region and Selected Countries, 1980–2005 (in percent).

Region	Inward Stock				Outward Stock			
	1980	1990	2000	2005	1980	1990	2000	2005
Developed economies	76.5	80.0	69.5	71.3	87.5	91.8	86.4	86.9
European Union	42.5	42.9	37.6	44.4	37.2	45.0	47.1	51.3
United States	14.8	22.1	21.7	16.0	37.7	24.0	20.3	19.2
Japan	0.6	0.6	0.9	1.0	3.4	11.2	4.3	3.6
Developing economies	23.5	19.9	29.2	26.2	12.5	8.2	13.2	11.9
Africa	6.9	3.3	2.6	2.6	1.3	1.1	0.7	0.5
America	6.2	5.8	8.3	8.2	8.4	3.3	3.0	3.2
Asia	10.2	10.7	18.3	15.3	2.9	3.8	9.5	8.2
China	0.2	1.2	3.3	3.1	…	0.2	0.4	0.4
India	0.1	0.1	0.3	0.4	0.0	0.0	0.0	0.1
ASEAN	3.4	3.5	4.5	3.7	0.2	0.6	1.4	1.6
Indonesia	0.8	0.5	0.4	0.2	0.0	0.0	0.1	0.1
Malaysia	0.9	0.6	0.9	0.5	0.0	0.1	0.4	0.4
Philippines	0.2	0.2	0.2	0.1	0.0	0.0	0.0	0.0
Singapore	1.0	1.7	1.9	1.8	0.1	0.4	0.9	1.0
Thailand	0.2	0.5	0.5	0.6	0.0	0.0	0.0	0.0
Vietnam	0.3	0.1	0.4	0.3	…	…	…	…
World	100.0	100.0	100.0	100.0	100.0	100.0	100.0	100.0

Region	Inflows				Outflows			
	1978–1980	1988–1990	1998–2000	2003–2005	1978–1980	1988–1990	1998–2000	2003–2005
Developed economies	81.0	82.7	78.2	60.8	44.8	50.6	64.4	54.6
European Union	39.1	40.3	46.0	40.7	39.7	13.6	15.9	15.7
United States	23.8	31.5	24.0	12.6	4.9	19.7	2.6	4.9
Japan	0.4	0.0	0.8	0.8	2.8	6.8	8.3	12.8
Developing economies	19.0	17.3	20.9	34.5	1.0	0.4	0.2	0.2
Africa	2.0	1.9	1.0	3.0	0.9	0.9	3.0	4.0
America	11.7	4.9	8.8	10.1	0.9	5.6	5.1	8.6
Asia	5.1	10.3	11.0	21.3	0.1	4.5	4.3	5.9
China	0.1	1.8	3.9	8.5	…	0.4	0.2	0.6
India	0.1	0.1	0.3	0.8	0.0	0.0	0.0	0.2
ASEAN	4.4	4.9	2.3	3.8	0.4	0.6	0.7	1.5
Indonesia	0.7	0.4	−0.2	0.3	0.0	0.0	0.0	0.3
Malaysia	1.5	0.9	0.3	0.5	0.4	0.1	0.1	0.3
Philippines	0.2	0.4	0.2	0.1	0.2	0.0	0.0	0.0
Singapore	1.8	2.2	1.3	2.1	0.2	0.5	0.5	0.8
Thailand	0.2	1.0	0.5	0.3	0.0	0.0	0.0	0.0
Vietnam	0.0	0.0	0.1	0.2	0.0	0.0	0.0	0.0
World	100.0	100.0	100.0	100.0	100.0	100.0	100.0	100.0

Source: UNCTAD FDI/TNC database.

to selected ASEAN economies, India, and China, respectively using bilateral FDI data from UNCTAD.[2,3]

Before proceeding with the analysis, it might be instructive to say a few words on the official definition of FDI and data sources to be used. The most common definition of FDI is based on the OECD *Benchmark Definition of FDI* (OECD, 1996, 3rd edn.) and IMF *Balance of Payments Manual* (IMF, 1993, 5th edn.). According to this definition, FDI generally bears two broad characteristics. First, as a matter of convention, FDI involves a 10% threshold value of ownership.[4]

Second, FDI consists of both the initial transaction that creates (or liquidates) investments as well as subsequent transactions between the direct investor and the direct investment enterprises aimed at maintaining, expanding or reducing investments. More specifically, FDI is defined as consisting of three broad aspects, viz. new foreign equity flows (which is the foreign investor's purchases of shares in an enterprise in a foreign country), intra-company debt transactions (which refer to short-term or long-term borrowing and lending of funds including debt securities and trade credits between the parent company and its affiliates) and reinvested earnings (which comprises the investor's share of earnings not distributed as dividends by affiliates or remitted to the home country, but rather reinvested in the host country). New equity flows could either take the form of M&A of existing local enterprises or Greenfield investments.

For ASEAN economies, there are three comprehensive databases on FDI inflows and outflows: IMF–BoP Manual, UNCTAD, and ASEAN Secretariat FDI Statistics.[5] UNCTAD and ASEAN by far have the most complete FDI database, and unlike the IMF–BOP data, they compile data on *bilateral*

---

[2]In this study, we are not concerned with bilateral FDI flows between China to India, and vice versa.

[3]Our selected ASEAN economies are Indonesia, Malaysia, the Philippines, Singapore, Thailand, and Vietnam.

[4]This said, the 10% threshold is not always adhered to by all countries systematically. For a detailed overview of the FDI definitions and coverage in selected developing and developed countries, see IMF (2003). Also see Duce (2003). UNCTAD (2007) discusses data issues pertaining to FDI inflows to China.

[5]See Duce (2003) for a comparison of IMF and UNCTAD and http://www.aseansec.org/18177.htm for ASEAN Secretariat FDI database.

FDI flows — both inflows and outflows. For this study, we chose to use UNCTAD data because unlike ASEAN Secretariat data, it is based on actual flows rather than appropriations. In addition, the ASEAN Secretariat data is only limited to the manufacturing sector. The main sources for UNCTAD's FDI flows are national authorities (central banks or statistical offices). These data are further complemented by data obtained from other international organizations such as the IMF, the World Bank, the Organization for Economic Co-operation and Development (OECD), the Economic Commission for Europe (ECE) and the Economic Commission for Latin America and the Caribbean (ECLAC), and UNCTAD's own estimates.

The remainder of the chapter is organized as follows. Section 5.2 discusses broad patterns and trends in intra-ASEAN FDI flows and flows between ASEAN and the rest of the world using bilateral net FDI flows over the period 1993–2005. Section 5.3 employs an augmented gravity model framework to examine the main determinants of regional FDI flows using bilateral data based over a period 1990–2004 on a panel dataset. We examine a range of drivers of FDI flows, including macroeconomic variables, transactional distance, institutional quality, and financial variables. Finally, Section 5.4 offers a few concluding remarks.

5.2 ASEAN FDI Flows: Trends and Patterns

One could analyze FDI data on either *stocks* (i.e., International Investment Positions) or *flows* (i.e., financial account transactions) data. While much empirical analysis to date has been undertaken using the former, changes in stocks could arise either because of net new flows or because of valuation changes and other adjustments (such as write-offs, reclassifications etc.). To abstract from these valuation and other changes, we consider only data on flows of inward FDI (net increases in).

5.2.1 *FDI flows between ASEAN and the rest of the world*

Table 5.3 focuses specifically on FDI inflows and outflows of selected ASEAN economies, China and India, between 1990 and 2005. Between 1990 and 1996, FDI inflows to ASEAN grew at an average annual rate of just over US$19 billion, while outflows grew at a rate of US$6.6 billion during

Issues in Governance, Growth and Globalization in Asia

Table 5.3. FDI Inflows and Outflows of Selected ASEAN Countries, China and India (US$ billions).

Country	1990–1996	1997–2005	1997	1998	1999	2000	2001	2002
Inflows								
World	248.3	816.2	489.7	712.0	1099.9	1409.6	832.2	617.7
Asia (excluding Japan)	51.3	114.6	100.4	91.1	108.7	143.8	104.0	88.6
ASEAN	19.3	25.2	34.3	22.3	28.8	23.5	19.5	15.8
Indonesia	2.7	0.2	4.7	−0.2	−1.9	−4.6	−3.0	0.1
Malaysia	5.0	3.5	6.3	2.7	3.9	3.8	0.6	3.2
Philippines	1.1	1.2	1.2	1.8	1.2	2.2	0.2	1.5
Singapore	6.7	13.6	13.8	7.3	16.6	16.5	15.6	7.3
Thailand	2.1	3.6	3.9	7.5	6.1	3.4	3.9	0.9
Vietnam	1.1	1.5	2.6	1.7	1.5	1.3	1.3	1.2
China: Mainland	22.8	50.9	45.3	45.5	40.3	40.7	46.9	52.7
India	1.0	4.4	3.6	2.6	2.2	3.6	5.5	5.6
Inflows			29.9	20.7	27.4	22.6	18.6	14.4
World	269.7	776.3	483.1	694.4	1108.2	1244.5	764.2	539.5
Asia (excluding Japan)	29.1	50.1	51.2	31.7	39.9	80.7	48.4	33.8
ASEAN	6.6	10.4	14.5	3.4	10.0	8.2	20.8	4.6
Indonesia	0.9	0.8	0.2	0.0	0.1	0.2	0.1	0.2
Malaysia	1.4	1.7	2.7	0.9	1.4	2.0	0.3	1.9
Philippines	0.2	0.2	0.1	0.2	0.1	0.1	−0.1	0.1
Singapore	3.6	7.4	10.9	2.2	8.0	5.9	20.2	2.3
Thailand	0.4	0.3	0.6	0.1	0.3	0.0	0.3	0.1
Vietnam	...	...	...	...	...	...	...	...
China: Mainland	2.3	3.4	2.6	2.6	1.8	0.9	6.9	2.5
India	0.1	0.9	0.1	0.0	0.1	0.5	1.4	1.7

Source: UNCTAD FDI/TNC database.

the same period. Buoyant global economic conditions and the liberalization of most of the ASEAN economies in the early 1990s led to an influx of inflows to the region. Despite the crisis, FDI inflows continued to rise during the period 1997–2004 at an average annual rate of US$23.7 billion, while FDI outflows also rose to an average annual rate of US$10 billion.

Not surprisingly, Singapore has the highest magnitudes of inflows and outflows among ASEAN countries. In both our sample periods 1990–1996 and 1997–2005, Singapore has been the single largest destination of FDI, accounting for between one-third and one-half of inflows to ASEAN during the last 15 years. More specifically, for the period 1990–1996, the average

FDI inflows to Singapore was around US$6.7 billion, while for the second sub-period, 1997–2005, the average FDI inflows to Singapore crossed US$13.5 billion. With regard to outflows, Singapore is clearly the single largest source of FDI outflows from ASEAN. FDI outflows from Singapore averaged at US$3.6 billion annually in the first sub-period and roughly at US$7.4 billion in the second sub-period. Referring to Table 5.3, it is apparent that Singapore, as the only Newly Industrializing Economies (NIE) in ASEAN, has consistently remained among the top developing economy sources of FDI over the last two decades. Malaysia (a near-NIE) is also notable for the size of their outward FDI flows, particularly since the 1990s.[6]

5.2.2 *Intra-ASEAN FDI flows*

Having considered broad country aggregate outflows and inflows to and from ASEAN, we analyze bilateral FDI between ASEAN economies. This exercise is far from straightforward. UNCTAD data on inflows and outflows do not match exactly (also see UNCTAD, 2006, Chapter 3). It is apparent that UNCTAD FDI outflows data from donor countries are incomplete for many countries. While some donor countries have relatively complete out-flows data, others either have incomplete data or no data at all. Different reporting practices of FDI data create bilateral discrepancies between FDI flows reported by home and host countries, and the differences can be quite large. For example, data on FDI flows to China as reported by the Chinese authorities and by the investing countries' authorities differ by roughly US$30 billion in 2000, US$8 billion in 2001, and US$2 billion in 2002.[7] Faced with these concerns, we draw inferences on FDI outflows by exam-ining FDI inflow data reported in the host economies as they are more complete and are available for all developing Asian economies under con-sideration. In other words, we focus on the *sources of inflows* rather than *destination of outflows*. To keep the analysis manageable, we examine data

---

[6]While there is not necessarily a one-to-one link between nationality of TNCs and FDI outflows, it is instructive to note that the handful of firms from ASEAN economies that made the Top 100 list were from Singapore and Malaysia.

[7]Apart from round-tripping and trans-shipping issues, part of the data inconsistencies between inflows and outflows arise because many countries do not include retained earnings or loans when considering FDI outflows.

for the averages of 1997–2000, and 2001–2004 rather than on an annual basis.[8]

FDI inflows between ASEAN countries in the post-1997 financial crisis (from 1997 to 2000) on average declined to 6.1% from the average of 7.1% before the crisis. However, robust economic growth and relatively low asset values led to a surge of FDI inflows between the member countries which in turn increased the average to 13.6% in the period 2001–2004. This increase in FDI inflows was even more pronounced in the year 2001, when intra-ASEAN contributed to one-fourth of FDI inflows to the region. After the 1997 financial crisis, the magnitude of FDI inflows between ASEAN countries has accounted for about one-eighth of all FDI inflows to the region (see Table 5.4), and is particularly pronounced from Singapore to the rest of ASEAN economies. According to Table 5.5, the average of FDI flows from Singapore to Malaysia from 1997 to 2005 has been around US$1 billion and accounts for almost 50% of intra-ASEAN. Bilateral flows from Singapore to Thailand are also significant during the same period with an average of close to US$1 billion.

FDI outflows and inflows for most countries under consideration during the sub-periods 1990–1996 and 1997–2005 are positively correlated, with the exceptions of ASEAN in general (second sub-period), Thailand (first sub-period), and the Philippines (second sub-period). The correlations in Indonesia, Malaysia, Mainland China and India are particularly high, suggesting that periods of economic liberalization have been characterized by simultaneous rises in both FDI inflows as well as outflows (see Table 5.6).

5.3 Determinants of FDI Flows

The previous section has highlighted the extent of FDI flows between ASEAN countries and more specifically, the intensification of intra-ASEAN FDI flows. But what explains the rise of intra-ASEAN FDI flows? This section undertakes a simple empirical investigation of some of the possible

---

[8]It is instructive to note that the top destinations of FDI using data based on FDI inflow data in host economy and FDI outflow data from donor economy have roughly stayed the same during the period under consideration.

Intra-ASEAN FDI Flows and the Role of China and India 77

Table 5.4. Average of Intra-ASEAN Bilateral Net FDI Flows (US$ Millions).

	Host								
	(1993–1996)			(1997–2000)			(2001–2004)		
	ASEAN	China	India	ASEAN	China	India	ASEAN	China	India
Source									
ASEAN	*1742.3*	*2136.4*		*1647.5*	*3438.7*	*22.0*	*2740.5*	*2983.2*	*43.0*
Brunei Darussalam	39.4	0.8		25.1			11.1		
Cambodia	1.7	0.7		0.5			3.1		
Indonesia	36.0	97.7		142.6	115.0		34.5	134.0	
Lao PDR	2.2			2.6			−0.5		
Malaysia	31.5	183.8		−23.5	290.8		−67.8	316.7	
Singapore	1598.2	1441.2		1374.7	2706.3	22.0	2750.2	2136.7	43.0
Philippines	14.2	122.9		48.6	135.9		55.0	212.2	
Thailand	18.2	269.8		72.3	185.8		−77.2	183.7	
Vietnam	1.0	19.5		4.6	4.9		31.9		
Mainland China	27.3			66.5			117.6		
India	2.8	1.9		39.8			31.1		
World	23909.9	35131.9		27222.3	42938.3		20212.2	53438.9	5289.5

Source: UNCTAD FDI/TNC Database.

Table 5.5.   Top 7 Bilateral Flows between ASEAN Countries[a] (US$ Millions).

Source	Host	Average		In percent to Total Intra-ASEAN FDI Inflow	
		(1997–2000)	(2001–2005)	(1997–2000)	(2001–2005)
Singapore	Malaysia	844.1	1273.3	51.2	46.5
Singapore	Thailand	441.7	1381.9	26.8	50.4
Singapore	Philippines	88.9	95.0	5.4	3.5
Indonesia	Singapore	104.5	16.1	6.3	0.6
Philippines	Thailand	4.9	48.4	0.3	1.8
Indonesia	Malaysia	26.0	15.8	1.6	0.6
Malaysia	Thailand	19.4	21.2	1.2	0.8

Source: UNCTAD FDI Database.
Note: [a]Based on FDI inflow data in host economy.

Table 5.6.   Correlations between Inflows and Outflows to and From Asia.

Country	1990–1996	1997–2005
Asia (excluding Japan)	0.99	0.80
ASEAN	0.81	−0.04
Indonesia	0.10	0.57
Malaysia	0.75	0.82
Philippines	0.68	−0.08
Singapore	0.9	0.46
Thailand	−0.02	0.07
Vietnam[a]	…	…
China: Mainland	0.24	0.61
India	0.94	0.88

Sources: Authors' calculations.
Note: No data on outflows.

determinants of FDI outflows from ASEAN to the rest of ASEAN, as well as flows between ASEAN–China and ASEAN–India over the period 1997–2004.[9] Can a gravity model framework that is commonly used to

---

[9]While we have FDI data until 2005, some of the independent variables are truncated at 2004.

rationalize outward FDI flows from OECD economies be used to understand intra-regional FDI flows in ASEAN?

5.3.1 *The model*

The aim of this section is to develop a relatively parsimonious model which includes commonly-used determinants as well as focus on specific bilateral variables. To this end, we follow the basic gravity-type framework which argues that market size and distance are important determinants in the choice of location of direct investment's donor countries. The theoretical basis for a gravity model of FDI has recently been proposed by Head and Ries (2008). The model has been used in a host of papers with some variations.[10]

The basic specification of our estimated model is outlined below:

$$\ln(\text{FDI}_{ijt}) = \beta_0 + \beta_1 \ln(\text{GDP}_{jt}) + \beta_2 \ln(\text{GDP}_{it}) + \beta_3 \ln(\text{DIST}_{ij})$$
$$+ \beta_4 X_{ijt} + \beta_5 \text{ASEAN}_{ij} + \mu_{ij} + \lambda_t + \nu_{ijt},$$

where FDI_{ijt} is the FDI outflow from source country (i) to host country (j) in time (t); GDP_{it} and GDP_{jt} are nominal Gross Domestic Products (GDPs) for the source country (i) and the host country (j) in time (t); DIST_{ij} is the geographical distance between host and source countries' capital cities; X_{ijt} is a vector of control variables influencing FDI outflows; ASEAN_{ij} is a binary variable equal to one if the bilateral FDI flows are between ASEAN countries and zero if the flows are between ASEAN and China or ASEAN and India, and vice versa; μ_{ij} denotes the unobservable country-pair individual effects; λ_t denotes the unobservable time effects (we use year dummies); and ν_{ijt} is a nuisance term.

The set of control variables comprises: lag of exports from country i to country j; volatility of exchange rate of i with respect to j (constructed by first taking the log difference of end-of-month exchange rates and then calculating a five-year rolling standard deviation), nominal exchange rate of

---

[10]The augmented gravity model for FDI is broadly similar — but by no means identical — to those used in recent papers including Lougani *et al.* (2002), Stein and Daude (2007), Liu *et al.* (2007). di Giovanni (2005) applies a gravity model to analyze cross-border M&A transactions.

i with respect to *j*; lag of the ratio of market capitalization to GDP in country *i*, contemporaneous ratio market capitalization to GDP of country's *j* stock market, and a political risk index in country *j*.

We expect the coefficients of the GDP of both the source and destination countries to be positive, as they proxy for masses which are important in gravity models.[11] As for the control variables, the sign for distance from donor to host country should be negative, as a greater distance makes a foreign operation more difficult and expensive to supervise and might therefore discourage FDI.[12] The effect of exports and FDI is ambiguous as FDI can either be a substitute or complement to trade in goods, implying ambiguity in its sign.[13] Volatility of exchange rate has no definite impact on the bilateral FDI flows since the effect ultimately depends on different empirical questions.[14] The bilateral nominal exchange rate which is measured in terms of the host country, should have a positive sign as a depreciated exchange rate in the host country should raise FDI inflows from the source country (due to the wealth effects). However, there are other channels that could lead to ambiguity of the signage (Cushman, 1985).

Financial depth plays a prominent role in international financial integration (for instance, see Demirgüç-Kunt and Levine, 2001). We use stock market capitalization in the country of the origin as a proxy for source of finance for firms to invest abroad. The sign on stock market capitalization in country *i* (lagged one period) ought to be positive for two reasons. One, higher stock market capitalization may have a positive wealth effect, hence

---

[11]In physics, the law of gravity states that the force of gravity between two objects is proportional to the product of the masses of the two objects divided by the square of the distance between them. Most gravity models in bilateral trade and FDI have replaced the force of gravity with the value of bilateral trade or direct investments and the masses with the source and destination countries' GDP.

[12]However, if the foreign firm is looking to service the host country's market, a longer distance also makes exporting from donor countries more expensive and might therefore make local production more desirable and encourage investment. This argument is not unlike the tariff-jumping one.

[13]We lag the exports variables by one period to account for endogeneity.

[14]Questions such as how involved the fixed costs in the acquisitions of a firm can go in two different ways, i.e., higher volatility will lead to less inflows yet higher volatility can also lead to more inflows since expected future cash flows from the target firm is correlated with liquid assets.

stimulating overseas acquisitions. Two, higher stock market capitalization could suggest that the source country firms have the ability to raise the funds to finance overseas ventures (di Giovanni, 2005). We also test how financial depth of the host country impacts the bilateral FDI flows to them. One of the ways FDI flows into the country is through merger and acquisition (M&A) activities. According to a research firm Dealogic, the value of global M&A activities for 2006 reached an all-time high of roughly $3.4 trillion, beating the previous record of $3.3 trillion in 2000. Low interest rates, strong stock market capitalization, and a more liberalized financial system in most emerging markets were reported as the main factors. Higher stock market capitalization in the host country could also be suggestive of general bullishness in and robustness of economic activity. However, the sign of this coefficient for the host country could be uncertain as there is a line of research suggesting that FDI tends to flow into countries with weaker financial systems, i.e., FDI is "bad cholesterol" (see Hausman and Fernández-Arias, 2000).

Anghel (2005) and Bénassy-Quéré *et al.* (2007) and Daude and Stein (2007) have discussed and explored in some detail the importance of institutional variables in determining FDI flows and Hur *et al.* (2007) have analyzed the importance of institutions in the case of M&A deals. In view of this, we include the political risk index of the International Country Risk Group (ICRG) database — a higher index in country j should encourage FDI flow. Finally, the sign for intra-ASEAN dummy variable should be positive.

5.3.2 *Data, methodology and results*

Tables A.1 and A.2 summarize the data sources to be used. The FDI data are based on the *UNCTAD FDI/TNC* database. Nominal GDP in US dollar and nominal exchange rates are taken from the IMF's *World Economic Outlook* database. Exports between source and host countries are taken from the IMF's *Direction of Trade and Statistics* database. Data on distance of capital cities are taken from the CEPII.[15] Political risk index is taken from ICRG

---

[15]Available at http://www.cepii.fr/.

database. Data on the ratio of stock market capitalization to GDP is taken from the World Bank's *World Development Indicators* database.

In our sample, we have eight source countries and six host countries from 1990 to 2004.[16] The data contains a large number of missing variables. A missing variable for bilateral FDI may indicate either "unreported FDI", reflecting the fact that the two countries have chosen to report low FDI values as zero, or "no FDI", indicating no FDI flows between the two. After a thorough observation of our data, we feel that most of the missing variables in our dataset happen because of "no FDI". Following normal convention in treating missing variables in bilateral data (see Eichengreen and Irwin, 1995; Stein and Daude, 2007), we replaced the zero flows with one. This will make them zeros when we take their natural logs in our empirical analysis. In all of our estimations, we deal with the issue of censored data. The common approach to dealing with censored data is to run a Tobit model (for instance see Bénassy-Quéré *et al.*, 2007, Daude and Stein, 2007; Lougani *et al.*, 2002).[17] We follow di Giovanni (2005) by computing a Tobit model using the two-step procedure. First, a probit model is estimated for whether a deal is observed or not conditional on the same right-hand variables as in Eq. (1), and the inverse Mills ratio is constructed from the predicted values of the model. Second, a regression is run to estimate Eq. (1) including the inverse Mills ratio as a regressor.[18] We also all employ a country-pair fixed effect which Anderson and Marcouiller (2002) suggest to be important (also see Eichengreen and Tong, 2007).

Results are summarized in Table 5.7. As is apparent, four variables stand out. One, GDP of the host country is statistically and economically

---

[16]We found no data on bilateral net FDI inflows to Indonesia and Vietnam from other ASEAN economies or from China or India in UNCTAD TNC/FDI database within our sample period (between 1990 and 2004).

[17]Another alternative suggested by Silva and Tenreyo (2006) is to use the Poison pseudo maximum likelihood method. This methodology has been recently applied to FDI by Head and Ries (2008). Coe *et al.* (2007) suggest another log-linear estimation method to deal with this problem.

[18]The standard errors are corrected for heteroskedasticity and we use an estimated parameter of an exogenous variable (the inverse Mills ratio) in the second stage. See di Giovanni (2005) for details.

Table 5.7.   Gravity Equation.

Dependent Variable: ln of bilateral FDI Outflows	Regression (1)	Regression (2)
ln(GDP$_i$)	0.175	0.223
	(0.728)	(0.726)
ln(GDP$_j$)	2.537***	2.319***
	(0.763)	(0.753)
ln distance	−1.590**	−2.147***
	(0.707)	(0.476)
Lag of export of goods from i to j	−0.257	
	(0.253)	
Nominal exchange rate of i to j	−0.342	−0.306
	(0.380)	(0.379)
Volatility of exchange rate of i to j	−0.109	−0.076
	(0.198)	(0.199)
Lag of stock market capitalization to GDP in i	0.297	0.267
	(0.312)	(0.311)
Stock market capitalization to GDP in i	0.688**	0.717**
	(0.301)	(0.30)
Political risk in j	0.064**	0.063**
	(0.030)	(0.03)
Intra-ASEAN dummy	1.108	1.17
	(4.659)	(3.20)
Observations	355	356
Adjusted R-Squared	0.65	0.64

Source: Authors' calculations.
Notes: Robust at standard error in parentheses.
*Significant at 10%; **significant at 5%; ***significant at 1%.
Year dummies, country-pair dummies, inverse Mills ratio, and constant are not shown.

significant with the correct sign. Two, stock market capitalization in the source country positively impacts FDI flows, suggesting that financial depth in the host country attracts FDI. Three, the political risk variable enters with a positive sign and is statistically significant. A higher index value implies lower level of risk and stronger institutional quality. Four, the distance variable is statistically significant with the correct sign. Exports (lagged one period) enter with a negative sign, suggesting possible substitution effects between trade and FDI. Interestingly, the exclusion of exports raises the elasticity of distance, suggesting that the distance variable on its own may be capturing both transactional as well as informational distance *à la* Lougani *et al.* (2002). Among the other variables, GDP in the source country is positive but not statistically significant. The coefficients of exchange rate values and volatility are both negative, but neither is statistically significant. *A priori* this is not entirely surprising in view of the fact that theory suggests their impact on FDI could go either way. The intra-ASEAN dummy is positive but not significant.

5.4 Concluding Remarks

This chapter has investigated trends, patterns and drivers of intra-ASEAN FDI flows using bilateral FDI flows between ASEAN, China and India for the period 1990–2005. The data indicate that intra-ASEAN FDI flows appear to have intensified during the period post-1997 financial crisis, with a large part of these flows concentrated between Singapore and its neighboring countries, i.e., Malaysia and Thailand. The chapter finds that an augmented gravity model fits the data fairly well and is able to capture around 65% of the variations in existing intra-ASEAN FDI flows. We find that a larger host country size enhances the institution quality in the host country, and greater financial depth in the host country appears to facilitate bilateral FDI flows within Asia. The policy implications here are apparent. There also appears to be evidence that a shorter distance between countries tends to facilitate bilateral FDI flows. While it is unclear whether this variable is capturing actual "transactional distance" or "informational distance" between countries, what is clear is that it is highly premature to proclaim the "death of distance".

References

Anderson, J and D Marcouiller (2002). Insecurity and the pattern of trade: An empirical investigation. *Rev. Econ. Stat.*, 84, 342–352.

Anghel, B (2005). Do institutions affect foreign direct investment? Universidad Autonoma de Barcelona, mimeo, October.

Bénassy-Quéré, A, M Coupet and T Mayer (2007). Institutional determinants of foreign direct investment. *World Econ.*, 30, 764–782.

Coe, DT, A Subramanian and N Tamirisa (2007). The missing globalization puzzle: Evidence of the declining importance of distance. *IMF Staff Papers*, 5, 34–58.

Cushman, D (1985). Real exchange rate risk, expectations, and the level of direct investment. *Rev. Econ. Stat.*, 67, 297–308.

Daude, C and EH Stein (2007). The quality of institutions and foreign direct investment. *Econ. Pol.*, 19, 317–344.

Demirgüç-Kunt, A and R Levine (2001). Financial structure and economic growth: A cross-country comparison of banks, markets and development. In *Bank-Based and Market-Based Financial Systems: Cross-Country Comparisons*, A Demirgüç-Kunt and R Ross Levine (eds.), pp. 81–140. Cambridge, MA: MIT Press.

di Giovanni, J (2005). What drives capital flows? The case of cross-border activity and financial deepening. *J. Int. Econ.*, 65, 127–149.

Duce, M (2003). Definitions of foreign direct investment (FDI): A methodological note. Banco de Espana, mimeo, July.

Eichengreen, B and D Irwin (1995). Trade blocs, currency blocs and the reorientation of trade in the 1930s. *J. Int. Econ.*, 38, 1–24.

Eichengreen, B and H Tong (2007). Is China's FDI coming at the expense of other countries? *J. Japanese Int. Econ.*, 21, 153–172.

Hausman, R and E Fernández-Arias (2000). Foreign direct investment: Good cholesterol? Working Paper No. 417, Inter-American Development Bank.

Head, K and J Ries (2008). FDI as an outcome of the market for corporate control: Theory and evidence. *J. Int. Econ.*, 74, 2–20.

Hiratsuka, D (2006). Outward FDI from ASEAN and intraregional FDI in ASEAN: Trends and drivers. ASEAN-UNCTAD Annual Seminar on Key Issues of FDI: Outward FDI from Asia Session 1, UNCTAD and ASEAN.

Hur, J, R Parinduri and Y Riyanto (2007). Cross-border M&A inflows and the quality of institutions: A cross-country panel data analysis. Working Paper No. 2007/08, Singapore Centre for Applied and Policy Economics, National University of Singapore.

International Monetary Fund (IMF) (1993). *Balance of Payments Manual*, 5th edn. Washington D.C.: IMF.

International Monetary Fund (IMF) (2003). *Foreign Direct Investment Statistics: How Countries Measure FDI 2001*. Washington D.C.: IMF.

Liu, L, K Chow and U Li (2007). Determinants of foreign direct investment in East Asia: Did China crowd out FDI from her developing East Asian neighbours? *China and the World Economy*, May–June, 70–88.

Lougani, P, A Mody and A Razin (2002). The global disconnect: The role of transactional distance and scale economies in gravity equations. *Scottish J. Pol. Econ.*, 18, 526–543.

Organisation for Economic Co-operation and Development (OECD) (1996). *Benchmark Definition of FDI*, 3rd edn. Paris: OECD.

Razin, A, Y Rubinstein and E Sadka (2003). Which countries export FDI, and how much? Working Paper No. 10145, National Bureau of Economic Research (NBER).

Razin, A, E Sadka and H Tong (2005). Bilateral FDI flows: Threshold barriers and productivity shocks, NBER Working Paper No. 11639, National Bureau of Economic Research.

Santos, JMCS and S Tenreyro (2006). The log of gravity. *Rev. Econ. Stat.*, 88, 641–658.

Stein, EH and C Daude (2007). Longitude matters: Time zones and the location of foreign direct investment. *J. Int. Econ.*, 71, 96–112.

Sudsawasd, S and S Chaisrisawatsuk (2006). Tigers and dragons against elephants: Does the rising Chinese and Indian share in trade and foreign direct investment crowd out Thailand and other ASEAN countries? *Asia-Pacific Trade Invest. Rev.*, 2, 93–114.

United Nations Conference on Trade and Development (UNCTAD) (2006). *World Investment Report 2006* (United Nations: New York and Geneva).

United Nations Conference on Trade and Development (UNCTAD) (2007). Rising FDI into China: The facts behind the numbers. Investment Brief No. 2.

World Bank (2006). *Global Development Finance*. New York: Oxford University Press.

Appendix

Table A.1   Variables Included in the Dataset.

Variables	Source
FDI Outflows	UNCTAD FDI/TNC database
Nominal GDP in US dollar	World Economic Outlook, IMF
Exports of goods	Direction of Trade Statistics, IMF
Exchange Rate	International Financial Statistics, IMF
Market capitalization of	World Development Indicators, World Bank
listed companies	CEPII
Distance	ICRG
Political Risk Index	

Table A.2   Source and Host Economies in the Dataset.

Source	Host
China (Mainland)	China (Mainland)
India	India
Indonesia	Malaysia
Malaysia	Philippines
Philippines	Singapore
Singapore	Thailand
Thailand	
Vietnam	

Table A.3   Summary of Statistics.

Variable	Units	Observations	Mean	Std. Dev	Min	Max
Bilateral FDI flows from i to j	US$ millions	334	183.7	503.9	−91.5	3575.0
Nominal GDP country i	US$ billions	600	214.8	312.6	6.5	1931.6
Nominal GDP country j	US$ billions	600	270.6	365.7	36.8	1931.6
Distance between capital cities	Kilometers	600	2776.9	1322.5	315.5	5220.9

(*Continued*)

Table A.3   (*Continued*)

Variable	Units	Observations	Mean	Std. Dev	Min	Max
Lag of export from i to j	US$ millions	599	6.7	1.7	−0.3	10.2
Bilateral nominal exchange rate of i w.r.t. j	Nominal	600	513.6	1484.9	0.0	9610.7
Bilateral exchange rate volatility of i w.r.t. j	Nominal	600	0.0	0.0	0.0	0.2
Market capitalization of listed companies in i	Percent of GDP	536	0.7	0.7	0.0	3.3
Market capitalization of listed companies in j	Percent of GDP	594	0.8	0.7	0.0	3.3
Political risk index	100 = min; 0 = max	600	68.0	11.0	34.8	89.1
Intra-ASEAN	Dummy, 1 = yes	600	0.5	0.5	0	1

Chapter 6

Extent of Real Financial Integration in Asia: Some Patterns and Stylized Facts[1]

Tony Cavoli

6.1 Introduction

The extent of economic interconnections that exist between individual economies and within regional groups or clusters is an important and ongoing policy topic in the broader areas of international economics and finance. There are a plethora of contributions in this literature that examine the extent of integration by observing single measures — such as the existence of trade agreements, or customs union, or indeed the existence of convergence of prices or interest rates. Yet, very few papers consider a multitude of dimensions. This chapter represents an attempt to stimulate interest in this area. In doing so, we attempt to answer the following questions: What are the connections and sequence between trade and financial integration? How financially integrated are the Asian economies? The empirics in this chapter will essentially be limited to countries that constitute the Association of Southeast Asian Nations (ASEAN) plus three economies for the period 1990–2009 subject to data availability.

As is shown in Sec. 6.4, the chapter adopts a novel and very simple method of measuring real and financial market integration using the conventional parity conditions, relative purchasing power parity (RPPP) and uncovered interest parity (UIP). To our knowledge, using the parity conditions in this manner to derive bilateral and regional integration has

---

[1]This paper is based on, and builds upon Cavoli and Rajan (2009b).

not been attempted in the literature. As such, we regard this as a significant value addition to work on the topic of integration.

To preview the results briefly, we find that, overall, integration is generally higher after the Asian crisis but the results are quite close. The original ASEAN nations — Indonesia, Malaysia, the Philippines, Singapore and Thailand — seem to be more integrated with rest of Asia than other groups.

The chapter is organized as follows. Section 6.2 explores the economic issues and relationships surrounding the issue of integration. Section 6.3 reviews some measures of integration that are commonly used in the literature.[2] Section 6.4 presents some results examining the extent of financial and real integration in Asia. Finally, Sec. 6.5 concludes the chapter.

6.2 Connections between Integration and Possible Monetary Union

What are the connections between integration and the possibility of the formation of a monetary union? This thread of the literature appears to have been developed through the lens of trade integration. Consider the following: first, if exchange rate stability encourages trade, the formation of an exchange rate union will help establish the conditions for a welfare-generating trade agreement. By reducing transactions and information costs, a single currency may encourage further trade among partners in a regional trade agreement (RTA). By the same token, however, an RTA may be undermined by exchange rate instability amongst members. Currency misalignment or competitive devaluations may generate a protectionist backlash which goes against the purpose of the RTA and possibly even threatens its existence.

Second, the increased openness and intra-union trade encouraged by forming an RTA makes flexible exchange rates less appropriate and monetary integration more appropriate among partner countries.

Third, while the increased factor mobility that may be associated with forming a common market may substitute to some extent for trade amongst partner countries (as suggested by conventional trade theory), it may also

---

[2]Keeping in mind our empirics are limited by the data availability for emerging Asian economies.

substitute for exchange rate adjustment and therefore help to meet the criteria for an OCA.

Fourth, to the extent that a monetary union encourages intra-industry trade within the union, it may help not only to enhance the welfare gains from regional trade integration but also encourage the closer synchronization of business cycles that then helps, retrospectively, to justify the formation of the monetary union.

A number of implications follow from this analysis. If further European Union enlargement encourages greater industrial specialization based on factor intensity-driven comparative advantage, it does not necessarily follow that the historical trend observed by Frankel and Rose (1998) will carry forward into the future. At the same time, however, the effects of industry-based asymmetrical shocks could be offset by the reduced incidence of demand-side shocks associated with the closer coordination of macroeconomic policy. The implication of this is that the effects of integration on the synchronization of business cycles within the integrated area are difficult to predict *a priori* and *ex-ante*. Fortunately, the principal purpose in this chapter is not to pursue this particular issue, but merely to observe that there will be inter-connections between trade and monetary integration, and that the direction of these connections may run both ways. Trade integration and the formation of a common market may help to create conditions more suitable for monetary integration. Meanwhile, monetary integration may help to facilitate trade integration. It is in this context that some political actors and independent observers have been suggesting that monetary integration can take place in conjunction with or even precede trade regionalism.

6.3 Price-based Measures of Financial and Real Integration

While monetary integration may be the final step in regionalism, it is important to explore the nexus between financial and real sector integration. There is enormous literature on the measurement of financial and real integration and there exist a number of measures of integration [see Fig. 6.1; also see Corbett (2009)]. The first category refers to the price-based conditions involving mainly debt flows. These are largely embodied in the interest parity conditions, viz. the covered interest parity (CIP), the UIP, and the

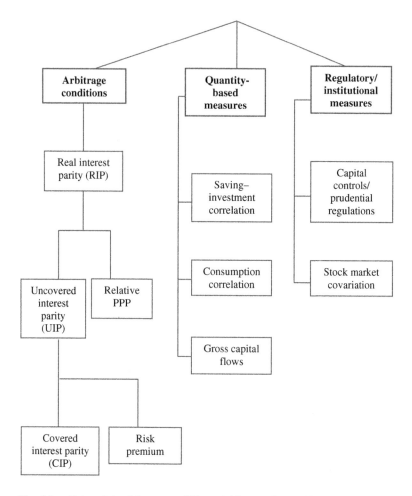

Fig. 6.1.   Categorizing Measures of Financial Integration: A Simple Framework.
Source: Cavoli and Rajan (2009a).

real interest parity (RIP). As will be discussed, the CIP is the narrowest of measures (of capital mobility *per se*), the UIP being a somewhat broader measure (of financial integration), while the RIP is the broadest of arbitrage measures incorporating both financial and real integration. The second category involves quantity-based measures, such as savings–investment correlations, consumption correlations, current account dynamics and gross capital flows.[3] The third category can be broadly classified as regulatory or institutional factors (such as capital controls and prudential regulations) as well as non-debt flows such as the co-movement of stock market returns. We limit our focus here to the common price-based measures [see Cavoli and Rajan (2009a), Chapter 9 for a discussion of quantity measures]. The aim is to formulate some stylized facts about the extent of financial integration amongst East Asian economies.

Price-based measures of financial integration or arbitrage conditions seek to equate rates of returns of comparable assets across different markets/economies. In this section, we examine three common interest parity conditions, viz. CIP, UIP and RIP.[4]

6.3.1 *The covered interest parity (CIP) condition*

The CIP may be formally stated as follows:

$$i_t = i_t^* + f_{t,t+n}^d, \tag{1}$$

where i_t is the domestic interest rate, i_t^* is the foreign or benchmark interest rate (US rate unless otherwise stated) and $f_{t,t+n}^d$ is the forward

---

[3]Gross capital flows and current account dynamics will not be covered here. See Montiel (1994) and Rajan and Siregar (2002) for the former and Obstfeld (1998) and Taylor (2002) for the latter. Also see Lane and Milesi-Feretti (2001). While examination of cross-border capital flows is useful, it is probably of limited use as a measure of financial integration. For instance, a country that is highly integrated with international capital markets — in the sense of there being no significant difference in domestic and international rates of return — will experience little if any international portfolio capital flows (at least debt related flows). An interesting extension to this issue is provided in McCauley *et al.* (2002) and McCauley (2007) who examine the extent to which Asian bonds issued are bought by Asian counterparties. Moreover, there is an interesting literature emerging where gravity-type models are being employed for financial flows as a way of measuring the likely direction of capital between countries [see Kim *et al.* (2006)].

[4]Another arbitrage condition is the closed interest parity condition which essentially states that the returns on identical instruments of the same currency but traded in different markets (such as onshore and offshore markets) should be equalized. Any deviation arising from this condition can be interpreted as possible evidence of the existence of capital controls in one of the two countries or the existence of other political or country risks that may prevent interest rate equalization. The measurement of the closed interest differential is difficult for developing economies as it requires that a particular asset is traded sufficiently for there to be a liquid offshore market for it (Obstfeld, 1998; Frankel and Okwongu, 1996).

margin (discount on the domestic currency) for n periods into the future (in logs).[5]

The CIP indicates that the difference between the current spot rate and the forward rate will equal the interest differential between similar assets measured in local currencies. Therefore, in the absence of capital account restrictions and/or transactions costs, the covered interest differential (CID) ought not to differ significantly from zero. A negative differential suggests the existence of capital controls or transactions costs that restrict capital *outflows*. Investors would certainly not tolerate a lower domestic return in the absence of capital controls (Frankel, 1991).

6.3.2 *The uncovered interest parity (UIP) condition*

The UIP may be represented as follows:

$$i_t = i_t^* + \Delta e_{t,t+n}^e, \tag{2}$$

where $\Delta e_{t,t+n}^e$ is the expected change in the log of exchange rate at time $t+n$.

The nexus between the UIP and the CIP is apparent by decomposing Eq. (2) as follows:

$$i_t - i_t^* - \Delta e_{t,t+n}^e = [i_t - i_t^* - (f_{t,t+n} - e_t)] + (f_{t,t+n} - e_{t,t+n}^e), \tag{3}$$

where the first bracketed term on the right-hand side is the CIP (sometimes referred to as country or political risk premium), and the second term is the currency risk premium. If the CIP holds but the UIP is rejected, this would imply that forward rates are biased predictors of future exchange rate.

Before formally testing Eq. (2), the researcher needs to find a way of measuring the expectation of the future exchange rate. One way to make the leap from theory to empirical operationalization is by using *ex-post* differentials. This may be justified by assuming that rational expectations (REs) hold. This assumption — that the actual or ex-post spot exchange rate equals the expected spot exchange plus an uncorrelated error term — is a practical way of overcoming the problem of non-observable expected

---

[5]Throughout this paper, the exchange rate is quoted as the domestic price of foreign currency. The forward margin can also be expressed as $(f_{t,t+n} - e_t)$ where $f_{t,t+n}$ is a forward rate and e_t is the spot rate (both in logs).

exchange rate changes. Another approach is to use surveys of exchange rate expectations of market agents.

6.3.3 *The real interest parity (RIP) condition*

The third arbitrage condition is the RIP. This condition may be derived by first taking the following UIP equation:

$$\Delta e^e_{t,t+n} = i_t - i^*_t \tag{4}$$

and substituting it into an expression for RPPP:

$$e_t = p_t - p^*_t \quad \text{or} \quad \Delta e^e_{t,t+n} = \pi^e_{t,t+n} - \pi^{e*}_{t,t+n}. \tag{5}$$

Combining the two with the Fisher equation, $r_t = i_t - \pi^e_{t,t+n}$ yields the expression for the RIP:

$$r_t = r^*_t. \tag{6}$$

Clearly for the RIP to hold the UIP, PPP and the Fisher hypothesis also need to simultaneously hold. This is no easy task given the lack of empirical success of both the UIP and PPP over the short to medium terms. Thus, the RIP is generally considered a very long-run interest parity condition encompassing both real and financial linkages.

6.3.4 *Summary of price-based measures*

The most popular methodology for determining the extent of financial integration is the UIP which was emphasized above. Indeed, as Flood and Rose have noted, "the UIP is a classic topic of international finance, a critical building block of most theoretical models..." (2002, p. 252). However, it is important to keep a number of caveats in mind when interpreting the findings. One, the test for the UIP is in fact a joint test for the CIP and the currency risk premium. We are unable to test separately for the CIP given the lack of data on forward foreign exchange markets in developing East Asia. Two, the tests for the UIP generally assume that all agents form expectations rationally. Thus, the failure of the UIP to hold [in the sense that there exists large and persistent uncovered interest differential (UIDs)], could be because: (1) the CIP does not hold (imperfect capital mobility), (2) there may be large and time-varying currency risk premia (imperfect asset substitutability (Bhatt and Virmani, 2005), or (3) RE is an inappropriate assumption for the foreign exchange markets (or that the market consists of heterogeneous agents).[6]

While the CIP is generally a preferred measure of financial integration in view of the preceding limitations of operationalizing the UIP (Frankel, 1991), as noted, there needs to be a liquid forward foreign exchange market in the currency pair under investigation. While this is not problematic for industrialized economies, it is definitely a niggling problem for developing economies. In any case, Willett *et al.* (2002) observe:

> Substantial deviations from covered interest parity are a good indication that capital mobility is less than perfect. However,...finding that covered interest parity holds..is consistent with either high or low capital mobility, and there is no good reason to presume that the magnitudes of deviations from interest parity will provide a reasonable proxy for the degree of international capital mobility. In terms of modern theory, the appropriate measure of capital mobility is the extent to which uncovered rather than covered interest parity holds (pp. 424–425).

With regard to the third price measure of financial integration, the RIP, the conditions for it to hold are quite prohibitive as both the PPP and the UIP need to simultaneously hold. However, the RIP provides a useful general condition encapsulating both trade and financial linkages, and thus should not be dismissed as being altogether irrelevant. The RIP is more likely to hold over longer time horizons and acts as a useful proxy for the marginal cost of capital.[7]

Whichever price measure of financial integration is used, there are two important considerations with their use. One, arbitrage conditions are probably a more appropriate way of measuring integration for certain sectors (e.g., the banking sector) rather than the whole economy (Chinn and Dooley, 1995). Two, a perennial problem with using such price measures,

---

[6]Also see Edwards and Khan (1985) and Willett *et al.* (2002).

[7]In fact, the UIP may also be more valid over longer time horizons, i.e., over one year (Madarassy and Chinn, 2002; Chinn and Meredith, 2004).

especially in developing economies, is what interest rate should be used, and to what extent the available interest rates are comparable across countries.

6.4 Integration in East Asia: Some Stylized Facts

6.4.1 *Measuring integration*

Integration will be measured by utilizing the parity conditions — UIP and RPPP. Both of these measures lend themselves appropriately as ways to ascertain the degree of integration between countries and they do so in a way that is underpinned by agent behavior in both the real and asset markets. However, since we are measuring integration and not the degree to which UIP and RPPP hold, the absolute value of the UID and RPPP (or, by construction, the real exchange rate) differential is taken. The UID is our proxy measure for financial market integration and the RPPP deviation represents our measure of real integration. These are given as follows:

$$\text{Real integration } (RI) = ABS(\Delta e^e_{t,t+n} + \pi^{e*}_{t,t+n} - \pi^e_{t,t+n}), \tag{7}$$

$$\text{Financial market integration } (FI) = ABS(i_t - i^*_t - \Delta e^e_{t,t+n}), \tag{8}$$

where the variables and notation are as described above. The *smaller the value of RI or FI, the greater is the possible integration* as a smaller number implies that the asset markets and/or goods markets exhibit greater convergence. An important caveat should be noted before proceeding.

There are, in this literature, many competing methods of calculating financial and real integration (Corbett, 2009). The rationale for selecting the ones described above are as because they are simple and easy to comprehend, data are available for all countries sampled (although the sample sizes do vary) and they are underpinned by economic intuition about agent behavior.

The two measures can be summed (or indeed averaged) and, thus, are able to be compared directly. This is crucial as we are examining the relationship and the interaction between the two measures.

6.4.2 *Data and sources*

Monthly observations for the period from 1990m1 to 2009m7 are used. All data are taken from the International Financial Statistics (IFS) CD database (August 2009) of the International Monetary Fund (IMF). Exchange rate data is taken from line RF and the cross rates were calculated from each local currency per US dollar. The exchange rates are reported in natural logs and, as such $\Delta e^e_{t,t+n}$ is calculated as (100*) the log monthly difference of the exchange rate. The interest rate data used is taken from line 60B, money market rates. These are based on interbank rates and contain sufficient volatility to form the basis of the empirical testing undertaken below. Interest rates are all divided by 12 to reflect a monthly return. Inflation data is taken from CPI series', line 64, and is calculated as the monthly change in CPI, $[\log \mathrm{CPI}(t) - \log \mathrm{CPI}(t-1)]*100$. Each measure, therefore, is a percentage absolute deviation from either RPPP or UIP.

Each measure of financial and real integration is calculated for each country pair and then each measure is calculated for each country against a regional grouping. The groupings (along with associated country acronyms) are as follows: ASEAN1 = [Indonesia (ID), Malaysia (MA), Philippines (PH), Singapore (SG), Thailand (TH)]. ASEAN2 = [Brunei (BR), Cambodia (CA), Laos (LA), Myanmar (MY), Vietnam (VT)]. ASEAN = ASEAN1 + ASEAN2. BIG3 = [China (CH), Japan (JP), Korea (KR)]. For example, we can measure Indonesia's integration (real and financial) with, say, Malaysia by observing the FI and RI between the two countries. We can also measure Indonesia's integration with the BIG3 by calculating her UID and Relative Purchasing Power Deviations (RPPD) with China, with Japan and with Korea. For these calculations, we simply added each bilateral measure, so Indonesia's level of financial integration with the BIG3 equals the FI between Indonesia and China + FI between Indonesia and Japan + FI between Indonesia and Korea. To derive the level of integration between a particular country and the region of which it is a member, the country is left out of the member's group.

6.4.3 *Results and discussion*

This section presents the extent of (or level of) *bilateral* integration by calculating the mean RI and FI for the full sample, a pre-Asia crisis sample and post-crisis sample. The second part examines how each country is integrated to a number of regional groupings.

Figures 6.2(a)–6.2(c) present the bilateral measures of integration by country for the full sample, pre-crisis and post-crisis samples respectively.[8] From these, we are able to extract information about the total level of integration for each country. Remember that the smaller the values, the higher would be the degree of economic connections. With regard to RI, integration generally appears to be higher post-crisis with India showing the greatest improvement. Singapore is highly integrated, and is so before and after the crisis while Myanmar is the least. The results are a little more spread for FI. Laos is the outlier for this measure, with low levels of FI — especially in the post-crisis period. Generally, post-crisis FI is lower than pre-crisis, in contrast to RI. Malaysia appears most integrated across time periods while China and Vietnam showed the most improvement in the post-crisis period.

Tables 6.1(a)–6.1(b) present the "top 5" in each measure of integration for each country for the complete sample. Tables 6.2(a)–6.2(b) present the top 5 for the pre-crisis period and Tables 6.3(a)–6.3(b) present the top 5 for the post-crisis period. Presenting the results this way allows us to assess the levels of integration after removing the outliers and allows us to detect any patterns in terms of which countries appear in the top 5 more often. We see that Malaysia and Singapore remain highly integrated for both RI and FI. In addition, India is also quite well integrated. With respect to the detection of any patterns, this is much less evident although a couple of general observations can be made. It would appear that for an original ASEAN country (ASEAN1), their top 5 would be more likely to comprise another ASEAN1 nation. The same can be said for the ASEAN2 countries. However, while there are several cases of ASEAN1 countries appearing in the top 5 of ASEAN2 ones, the opposite situation is less likely to occur. Even less likely is the appearance of ASEAN2 countries in the top 5 of the BIG3.

Given the above, we can now proceed to assess the levels of integration corresponding to regional groups. Figures 6.3(a)–6.3(c) present the extent

---

[8]To see the raw data for these bilateral measures, see Cavoli and Rajan (2009b).

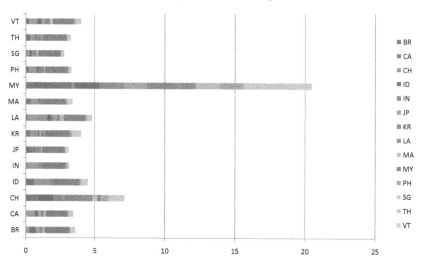

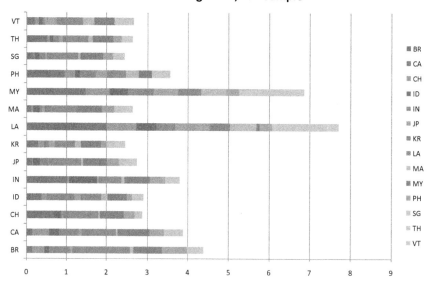

Fig. 6.2.   (a) Bilateral Integration by Country, Full Sample.

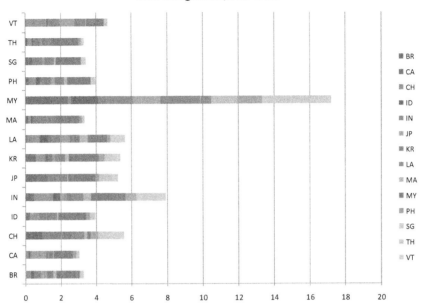

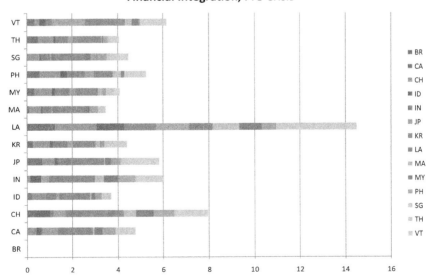

Fig. 6.2.   (b) Bilateral Integration by Country, Pre-Crisis.

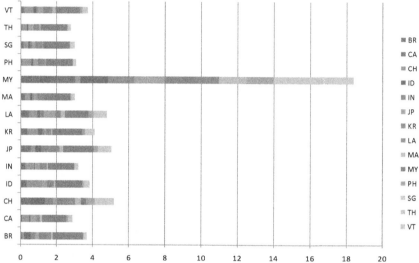
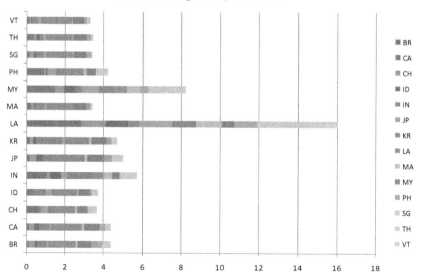

Fig. 6.2.   (c) Bilateral Integration by Country, Post-Crisis.

Table 6.1. (a) Top 5 Real Integration for Full Sample.

BR		CA		CH		ID		IN	
CA	0.003	BR	0.003	JP	0.062	MA	0.008	MA	0.013
SG	0.007	LA	0.015	SG	0.162	IN	0.021	VT	0.017
IN	0.052	IN	0.039	MY	0.195	KR	0.037	ID	0.021
LA	0.105	VT	0.076	BR	0.268	TH	0.056	TH	0.035
KR	0.112	PH	0.087	MA	0.385	JP	0.095	CA	0.039
	0.279		*0.22*		*1.072*		*0.217*		*0.125*

JP		KR		LA		MA		MY	
PH	0.022	MA	0.031	VT	0.012	ID	0.008	CH	0.195
SG	0.024	ID	0.037	CA	0.015	IN	0.013	VT	1.502
TH	0.038	IN	0.059	BR	0.105	KR	0.031	LA	1.55
CH	0.062	BR	0.112	SG	0.114	TH	0.046	CA	1.572
IN	0.073	JP	0.132	PH	0.143	JP	0.086	SG	1.644
	0.219		*0.371*		*0.389*		*0.184*		*6.463*

PH		SG		TH		VT	
SG	0.001	PH	0.001	IN	0.035	LA	0.012
JP	0.022	BR	0.007	JP	0.038	IN	0.017
TH	0.061	JP	0.024	MA	0.046	CA	0.076
CA	0.087	TH	0.063	ID	0.056	BR	0.158
IN	0.096	IN	0.098	PH	0.061	PH	0.178
	0.267		*0.193*		*0.236*		*0.441*

Table 6.1. (b) Top 5 Financial Integration for Full Sample.

BR		CA		CH		ID		IN	
JP	0.072	MA	0.039	JP	0.008	KR	0.02	CH	0.054
MA	0.084	JP	0.079	SG	0.027	TH	0.081	JP	0.054
SG	0.086	VT	0.079	MA	0.035	VT	0.082	MA	0.066
ID	0.108	SG	0.084	IN	0.054	BR	0.108	VT	0.066
KR	0.111	BR	0.149	TH	0.068	SG	0.12	KR	0.088
	0.461		*0.43*		*0.192*		*0.411*		*0.328*

JP		KR		LA		MA		MY	
CH	0.008	ID	0.02	MY	0.075	CH	0.035	LA	0.075
SG	0.044	TH	0.075	PH	0.307	CA	0.039	PH	0.314

(*Continued*)

Table 6.1. (*Continued*)

JP		KR		LA		MA		MY	
IN	0.054	IN	0.088	VT	0.398	JP	0.055	ID	0.472
MA	0.055	BR	0.111	IN	0.474	SG	0.065	KR	0.494
BR	0.072	SG	0.113	ID	0.483	IN	0.066	VT	0.503
	0.233		*0.407*		*1.737*		*0.26*		*1.858*

PH		SG		TH		VT	
VT	0	CH	0.027	SG	0.038	PH	0
ID	0.125	TH	0.038	CH	0.068	IN	0.066
KR	0.146	JP	0.044	KR	0.075	CA	0.079
TH	0.206	MA	0.065	ID	0.081	ID	0.082
SG	0.246	CA	0.084	JP	0.083	CH	0.091
	0.723		*0.258*		*0.345*		*0.318*

Table 6.2. (a) Top 5 Real Integration for Pre-Crisis Sample.

BR		CA		CH		ID		IN	
PH	0.018	MA	0.019	JP	0.026	JP	0.015	CA	0.106
VT	0.031	TH	0.021	SG	0.061	MA	0.053	KR	0.244
LA	0.035	BR	0.037	CA	0.117	TH	0.067	ID	0.382
CA	0.037	VT	0.046	MA	0.163	CA	0.071	BR	0.384
SG	0.082	ID	0.071	MY	0.178	VT	0.073	JP	0.398
	0.203		*0.194*		*0.545*		*0.279*		*1.514*

JP		KR		LA		MA		MY	
ID	0.015	ID	0.138	BR	0.035	TH	0.014	CH	0.178
CH	0.026	JP	0.153	CA	0.086	CA	0.019	VT	0.98
MA	0.038	MA	0.192	PH	0.181	VT	0.025	CA	1.08
TH	0.052	TH	0.206	SG	0.207	JP	0.038	LA	1.092
KR	0.153	IN	0.244	VT	0.267	ID	0.053	BR	1.323
	0.284		*0.933*		*0.776*		*0.149*		*4.653*

PH		SG		TH		VT	
BR	0.018	PH	0.055	MA	0.014	MA	0.025
SG	0.055	CH	0.061	CA	0.021	BR	0.031
VT	0.057	BR	0.082	VT	0.042	TH	0.042
TH	0.156	TH	0.1	JP	0.052	CA	0.046
MA	0.17	CA	0.106	ID	0.067	PH	0.057
	0.456		*0.404*		*0.196*		*0.201*

Table 6.2. (b) Top 5 Financial Integration for Pre-Crisis Sample.

CA		CH		ID		IN	
IN	0.039	IN	0.124	SG	0.072	CA	0.039
SG	0.045	VT	0.244	MA	0.073	CH	0.124
MA	0.093	CA	0.42	TH	0.085	VT	0.294
ID	0.217	SG	0.525	JP	0.124	JP	0.349
KR	0.267	MA	0.54	KR	0.134	MA	0.399
	0.661		*1.853*		*0.488*		*1.205*

JP		KR		LA		MA		MY	
MA	0.051	MY	0.011	PH	0.639	SG	0.001	KR	0.011
SG	0.051	TH	0.049	MY	0.977	TH	0.016	TH	0.059
ID	0.124	ID	0.134	KR	1.018	JP	0.051	ID	0.145
TH	0.209	PH	0.163	VT	1.031	ID	0.073	PH	0.153
KR	0.258	SG	0.207	MA	1.187	CA	0.093	SG	0.217
	0.693		*0.564*		*4.852*		*0.234*		*0.585*

PH		SG		TH		VT	
VT	0.048	MA	0.001	MA	0.016	PH	0.048
MY	0.153	CA	0.045	KR	0.049	CH	0.244
KR	0.163	JP	0.051	MY	0.059	ID	0.256
TH	0.213	ID	0.072	ID	0.085	IN	0.294
ID	0.298	TH	0.157	SG	0.157	MA	0.318
	0.875		*0.326*		*0.366*		*1.16*

Table 6.3. (a) Top 5 Real Integration for Post-Crisis Sample.

BR		CA		CH		ID		IN	
PH	0.014	ID	0.007	BR	0.132	CA	0.007	TH	0.02
TH	0.029	KR	0.022	JP	0.251	IN	0.034	ID	0.034
SG	0.035	IN	0.041	SG	0.255	TH	0.054	CA	0.041
CA	0.092	TH	0.062	TH	0.272	PH	0.084	PH	0.05
MA	0.124	VT	0.074	MY	0.275	MA	0.107	MA	0.074
	0.29		*0.21*		*1.19*		*0.29*		*0.22*

JP		KR		LA		MA		MY	
KR	0.105	CA	0.022	ID	0.139	SG	0.015	CH	0.275
SG	0.189	MA	0.069	CA	0.179	PH	0.023	LA	1.278

(Continued)

Table 6.3.   (a) (*Continued*)

JP		KR		LA		MA		MY	
MA	0.205	SG	0.084	VT	0.198	TH	0.049	VT	1.345
PH	0.229	JP	0.105	IN	0.221	KR	0.069	CA	1.382
BR	0.236	TH	0.118	TH	0.223	IN	0.074	IN	1.464
	0.96		*0.4*		*0.96*		*0.23*		*5.74*

PH		SG		TH		VT	
BR	0.014	MA	0.015	IN	0.02	CA	0.074
MA	0.023	BR	0.035	BR	0.029	IN	0.088
TH	0.029	PH	0.039	PH	0.029	TH	0.122
SG	0.039	TH	0.069	MA	0.049	ID	0.126
IN	0.05	KR	0.084	ID	0.054	BR	0.131
	0.16		*0.24*		*0.18*		*0.54*

Table 6.3.   (b) Top 5 Financial Integration for Post-Crisis Sample.

BR		CA		CH		ID		IN	
JP	0.073	VT	0.007	PH	0.04	VT	0.011	PH	0.071
MA	0.084	KR	0.044	ID	0.046	CH	0.046	CH	0.152
SG	0.086	JP	0.092	VT	0.117	MA	0.06	TH	0.189
ID	0.108	SG	0.092	MA	0.136	PH	0.086	VT	0.283
KR	0.111	TH	0.144	IN	0.152	BR	0.108	JP	0.321
	0.46		*0.38*		*0.49*		*0.31*		*1.02*

JP		KR		LA		MA		MY	
BR	0.073	SG	0.018	IN	0.555	VT	0.015	IN	0.326
CA	0.092	TH	0.018	MY	0.678	TH	0.035	PH	0.448
MA	0.155	CA	0.044	PH	1.149	SG	0.039	CH	0.484
KR	0.166	BR	0.111	ID	1.159	ID	0.06	VT	0.593
TH	0.184	MA	0.114	KR	1.238	BR	0.084	ID	0.603
	0.67		*0.31*		*4.78*		*0.23*		*2.45*

PH		SG		TH		VT	
CH	0.04	TH	0.001	SG	0.001	CA	0.007
IN	0.071	KR	0.018	KR	0.018	ID	0.011
ID	0.086	MA	0.039	MA	0.035	MA	0.015
VT	0.163	VT	0.082	VT	0.091	SG	0.082
MA	0.193	BR	0.086	ID	0.138	TH	0.091
	0.55		*0.23*		*0.28*		*0.21*

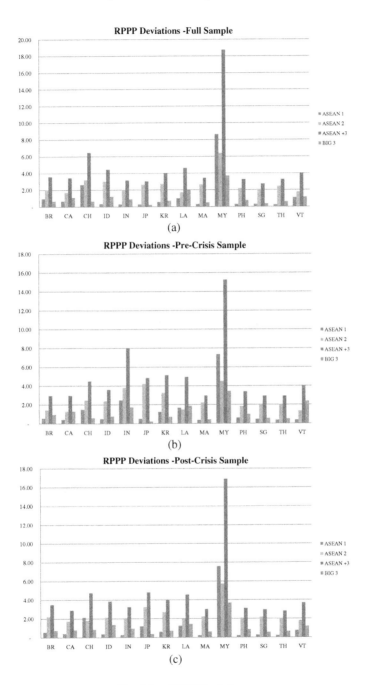

Fig. 6.3.   RPPP Deviations.

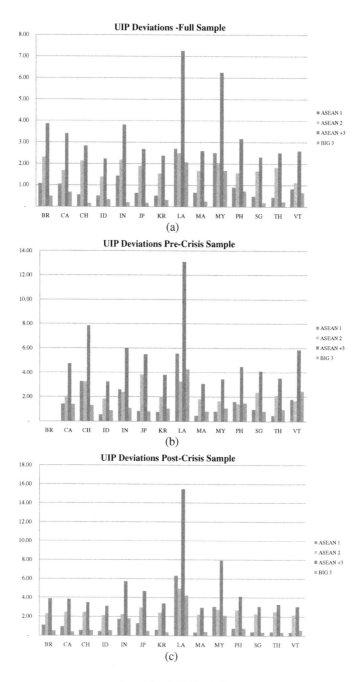

Fig. 6.4.   UIP Deviations.

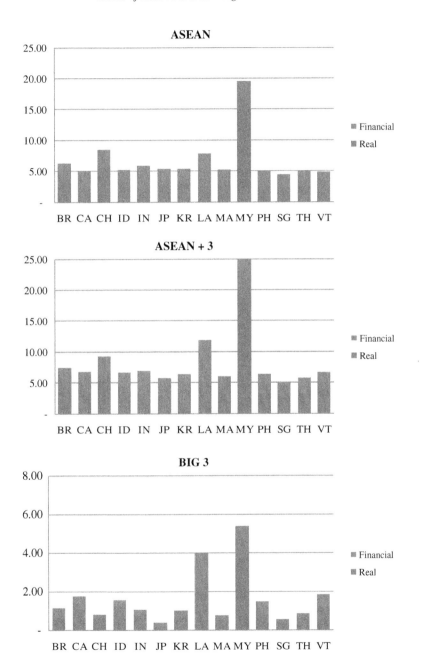

Fig. 6.5.   (a) Real + Financial Integration, Full Sample.

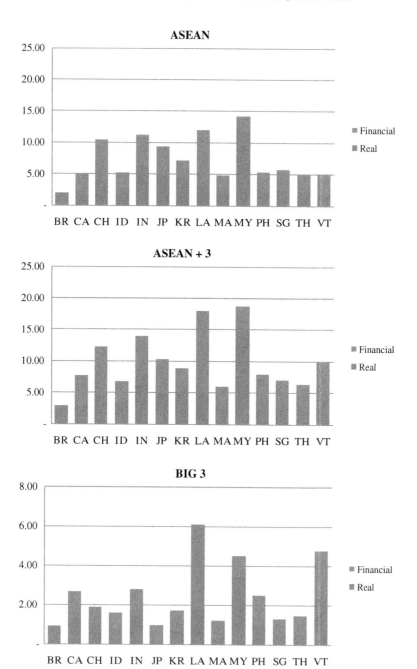

Fig. 6.5.   (b) Real + Financial Integration, Pre-Crisis.

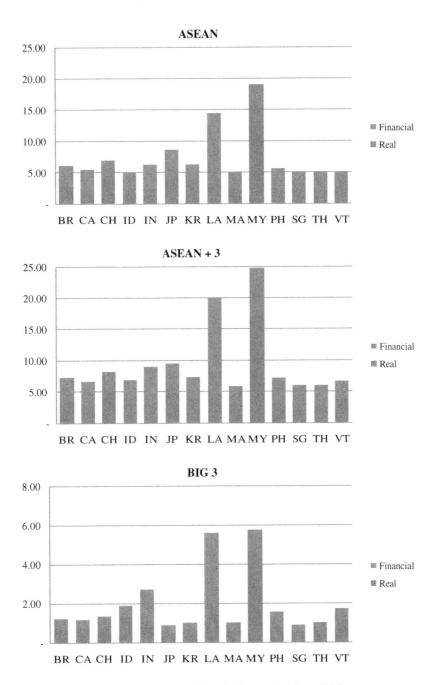

Fig. 6.5.   (c) Real + Financial Integration, Post-Crisis.

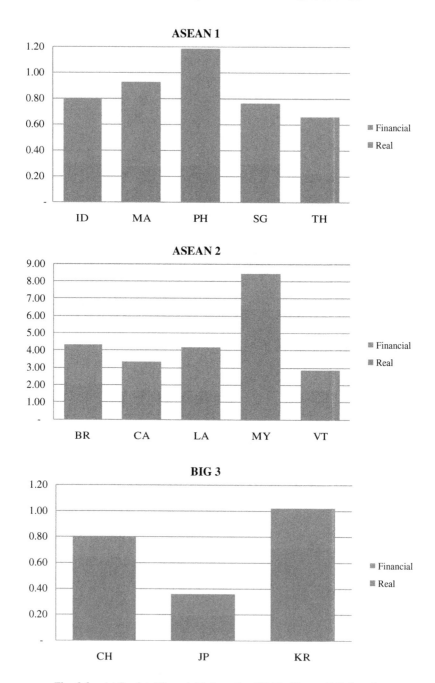

Fig. 6.6.   (a) Real + Financial Integration Within Group, Full Sample.

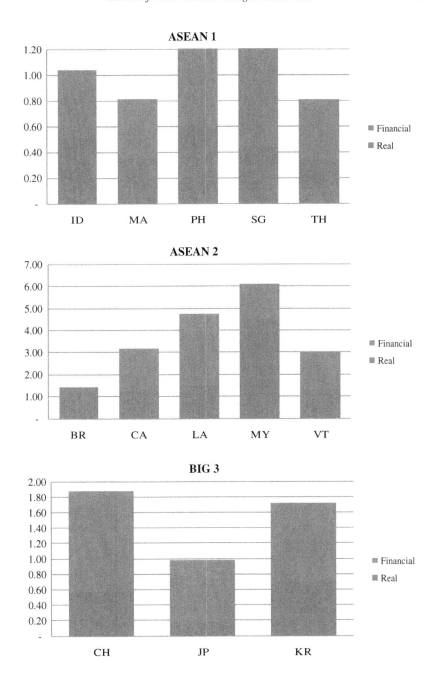

Fig. 6.6.   (b) Real + Financial Integration Within Group, Pre-Crisis Sample.

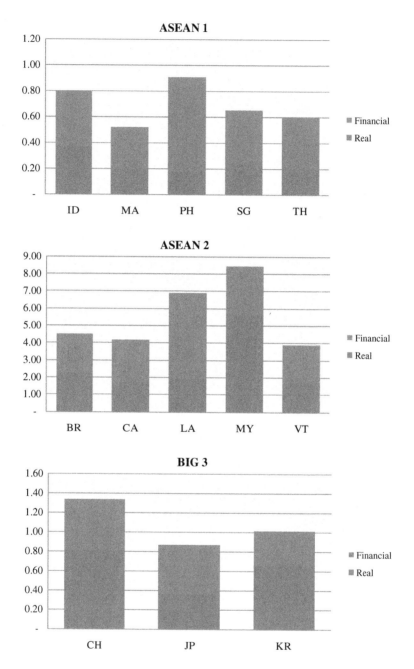

Fig. 6.6.   (c) Real + Financial Integration Within Group, Post-Crisis Sample.

of bilateral RI for each country to the groupings defined above for the full sample, pre-crisis and post-crisis samples respectively. The level of integration in the post-crisis sample appears to be marginally less (larger RI and FI) than the pre-crisis sample. The level of integration of Myanmar is lower than others — as seen in Figs. 6.1(a)–6.1(c). The RI to the ASEAN2 nations is lower (higher RI) than for other groupings.

Figures 6.4(a)–6.4(c) present the extent of bilateral FI for each country to the groupings defined above for the full sample, pre-crisis and post-crisis samples respectively. As with the results for RI, the differences appear minimal and the level of integration to ASEAN2 is lower than for the others.

Figures 6.5(a)–6.5(c) show the relationship between RI and FI by presenting both together (summed) as a measure of "economic" integration. This is done for each country as measured against ASEAN, ASEAN+3 and BIG3 for the full, pre-crisis and post-crisis samples respectively. It looks as though there is a lower degree of financial integration (larger FI value) post-crisis against ASEAN+3 than when compared to the pre-crisis — but the effect is quite marginal. The opposite appears to occur when the level of integration against ASEAN is observed, but it is again worth noting that the effect is slight. The extent of integration to the BIG3 countries is identifiably high.

Figure 6.6 shows the extent of economic (RI + FI) for each member of ASEAN1, ASEAN2 and BIG3 with its own group. It is quite clear here that real integration is greater than financial integration for the post-crisis period when one examines the results for ASEAN1 and BIG3. The results are less clear cut for ASEAN2, although the overall level of integration appears lower.[9]

6.5 Conclusion

The analysis undertaken in this chapter suggests that there is no obvious indication of intensified financial market integration in the East Asian region on the whole. Nonetheless, the evidence would appear to reveal a close correspondence between measures of financial integration and the extent of

---

[9]We cannot compare the results for Brunei due to data being unavailable for this sample period.

the development of financial markets in general in that, at a bilateral and regional level, those countries with greater financial integration (lower FI) tend to have more diversified deeper, larger financial markets.[10] The three East Asian financial centers, and high-income economies of Hong Kong,[11] Japan and Singapore are fairly highly integrated with global capital markets. The recent pace of liberalization in Korea post-crisis is also intensifying the country's extent of international financial integration. The lower middle-income Southeast Asian countries, Thailand, Indonesia and the Philippines are relatively less financially integrated, but still more integrated, in general, when one compares them to the less-developed ASEAN countries of Brunei, Cambodia, Laos, Myanmar and Vietnam.

The analysis of the extent and sequence of real versus financial market integration finds that, overall, integration is generally higher after the Asian crisis but the results are quite close. The original ASEAN nations seem to be more integrated with rest of Asia than other groups. This is the case for both real and financial integration and they tend to be especially well integrated with each other. It ought to be pointed out here that, whilst there is quite a lot of information presented in the pages above, there remains much scope for future research — particularly in the area of utilizing quantity-based integration measures. This would be useful for both showing robustness and for the additional information regarding integration contained in those measures. Furthermore, more formal testing using panel and VAR methods would uncover more information about the determinants of integration and on any possible sequencing that may have taken place.

While these countries continue with their ongoing liberalization efforts, one would expect their effective degree of financial integration to intensify over time. It has, however, been argued that these liberalization attempts may lead to enhanced *regional* rather than *global* integration (Eichengreen and Park, 2003; Park and Bae, 2002). While this a real possibility,[12] policy makers in East Asia have taken the view that there are positive externalities from cooperating to strengthen their individual financial sectors, to develop

---

[10]There is sizable literature on this topic. One of the most recent papers is Chinn and Ito (2005).

[11]Not examined in the empirical section in this work.

[12]However, see McCauley *et al.* (2002) for a counter argument.

regional financial markets, and in particular, to diversify their financial structures away from bank-based systems to bond markets. Motivated by this, a number of financial cooperation initiatives have been underway in East Asia, including the Asian Bond Fund (ABF) established by the 11 members of the Executives' Meeting of East Asia-Pacific Central Bank (EMEAP) and the Asian Bond Market Initiative (ABMI) by Asian Plus Three (APT) economies. The more successful are these early initiatives, and the deeper and broader they become over time, the greater is the likelihood that the region's financial systems will become more closely intra-regionally integrated.

References

Bhatt, V and A Virmani (2005). Global integration of India's money market: Interest rate parity in India. Working Paper No. 164, Indian Council for Research on International Economic Relation, New Delhi.

Cavoli, T and RS Rajan (2009a). *Exchange Rate Regimes and Macroeconomic Management in Asia*. HK: Hong Kong University Press.

Cavoli, T and RS Rajan (2009b). Sequencing and extent of integration in Asia: The real financial dimensions. In *ERIA Proceedings*, No. 1. Available at http://www.eria.org/pdf/research/y2009/no1/Ch02-DEI01.pdf. Accessed 12th January 2013.

Chang, LL and RS Rajan (2001). The economics and politics of monetary regionalism in Asia. *ASEAN Econ. Bull.*, 18, 103–118.

Chinn, MD and H Ito (2005). What matters for financial development? Capital controls, institutions and interactions. Working Paper 11370, NBER.

Chinn, MD and G Meredith (2004). Monetary policy and long-horizon uncovered interest parity. *IMF Staff Papers*, 51, pp. 409–30.

Chinn, M and M Dooley (1995). Asia-Pacific capital markets: Integration and implications for economic activity. Working Paper No. 5280, NBER.

Corbett, J (2009). Asian financial integration. Mimeo, Australian National University.

Edwards, S and M Khan (1985). Interest rate determination in developing countries. *IMF Staff Papers*, 32, 377–403.

Eichengreen, B and YS Park (2003). Why has there been less financial integration in Asia than in Europe? Mimeo (January).

Flood, R and A Rose (2002). Uncovered interest parity in crisis. *IMF Staff Papers*, 49, 252–265.

Frankel, J (1991). Quantifying international capital mobility in the 1980s. In *National Saving and Economic Performance*, B Bernheim and J Shoven (eds.). Chicago: University of Chicago Press.

Frankel, J and C Okwongu (1996). Liberalized portfolio capital inflows in emerging markets: Sterilization, expectations and the incompleteness of interest rate convergence. *Int. J. Finance Econ.*, 1, 1–23.

Frankel, J and A Rose (1998). The endongeneity of the optimum currency area criteria. *Econ. J.*, 108, 1009–1025.

Kim, S, J-W Lee and K Shin (2006). Regional and global financial integration in East Asia. Mimeo, May, Korea University.

Lane, PR and GM Milesi-Feretti (2001). The external wealth of nations: Measures of foreign assets and liabilities for industrial and developing countries. *J. Int. Econ.*, 55, 263–294.

Madarassy, R and M Chinn (2002). Free to flow? New results on capital mobility amongst the developed countries. Mimeo (August).

McCauley, RN (2007). Building an integrated capital market in East Asia. Discussion Paper No. 83, Asia Development Bank Institute, November.

McCauley, RN, SS Fung and B Gadanecz (2002). Integrating the finances of East Asia. *BIS Quart. Rev.*, December, 83–95.

Montiel, P (1994). Capital mobility in developing countries: Some measurement issues and empirical estimates. *World Bank Econ. Rev.*, 8, 311–350.

Obstfeld, M (1998). The global capital market: Benefactor or menace? *J. Econ. Persp.*, 12, 9–30.

Park, YC and KH Bae (2002). Financial liberalization and economic integration in East Asia. Paper presented at the PECC Finance Forum Conference on "Issues and Prospects for Regional Cooperation for Financial Stability and Development", Hawaii, 11–13 August.

Rajan, RS (2005). Asian economic cooperation and integration: Sequencing of financial, trade and monetary regionalism, in *Asian Economic Cooperation and Integration: Progress Prospects and Challenges*. Manilla: Asian Development Bank.

Rajan, RS and R Siregar (2002). Boom, bust and beyond. In *Financial Markets and Policies in East Asia*, G de Brouwer (ed.). London: Routledge.

Taylor, AM (2002). A century of current account dynamics. *J. Int. Money Finance*, 21, 725–748.

Willett, T, M Keil and YS Ahn (2002). Capital mobility for developing countries may not be so high. *J. Develop. Econ.*, 68, 421–434.

Chapter 7

The Global Financial Crisis, Rise of China, and Changes in the Geographical Location of Control of Large Listed Companies

Ron McIver

7.1 Introduction

The objectives of this chapter are to provide an overview and some insights into the extent to which the global financial crisis (GFC) has altered the rate of change in the global economic and financial landscapes, particularly as these apply to the relative global position of the East Asian-Pacific region and, more specifically, China. In doing so it will also address the fact that, while the growth in China's (and, more generally, East Asia's) economic and financial resources and influence are well recognized, there has been less focus on East Asian, and particularly Chinese, control of large multinational corporations as a result of globalization. These large enterprises are important due to their dominance in determining both foreign direct investment (FDI) and trade flows.

To achieve its objective, this chapter presents data and discussion on changes in the geographic origin (control) and industry distribution of large (Top 500) listed companies over the period 2006–2009. That is, the time period immediately preceding the GFC and that covering it. This is done against the backdrop of measures of the relative economic [gross domestic product (GDP)] and financial (total market capitalization) position of major regions and countries covering the time period 1999–2009 to establish more recent trends, and which begins the discussion (see Appendix A for discussion of the sources of data).

7.2 The Rise of China and (Return) of East Asian Economic Power

It is now a commonplace to recognize the presence of a significant (and even accelerating) shift of global economic power to Asia, particularly China, and thus East Asia and the Pacific, as part of the process of globalization. Often discussed are shares in the value of global output [GDP or gross national income (GNI)] produced within countries and regions. At the same time, there is (perhaps incorrectly) acceptance of the decline of North America in terms of its economic and political influence. This is particularly in the East Asian region as a result of the decline in its share of global GDP and the rise in the presence of China (Breslin, 2009).

Although appearing rapid to many, China's gains in global economic position cannot be viewed as a sudden phenomenon. Rather they are a longer-term consequence of a gradual process of modernization in China and the internationalization of its economy. Thus, these gains reflect (among other factors): a rise in China's industrial competitiveness through the 1980s and 1990s associated with industrial reform (Zhao and Zhang, 2007), the opening of competition against state-owned enterprises (Imai, 2000), large inflows of FDI (Huang, 2003), and commercialization of its banking system (McIver, 2009).

Figure 7.1 provides data allowing some analysis of the shifting global shares of GDP (as measured in current US dollars). It is apparent from Fig. 7.1 that the share of global GDP sourced out of North America (and thus largely the US) has declined considerably since the early 2000s. However, rather than fall more rapidly as a result of the GFC, it would appear that the North American share of GDP has temporarily stabilized.

As Fig. 7.1 also apparently illustrates, much of the overall decline in the value of North America's (and the US's) share of global output over the 2000s can be explained by rises in output in the rest of the world (Latin America and the Caribbean, the Middle East and North Africa, South Asia, and Sub-Saharan Africa) and, in particular, an increase in the share of global GDP provided by Europe and Central Asia. However, over much of the period associated with the GFC, the global share of GDP of Europe and Central Asia fell, while that of the rest of the world stabilized. Finally, although the share of world income generated in the East Asian-Pacific

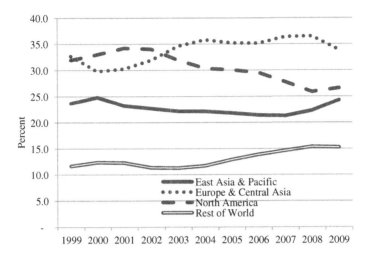

Fig. 7.1.   Regional Shares of GDP (% of World, Current US Dollars).
Source: World Bank, *World Development Indicators*, and author's calculations.

region has grown relatively strongly throughout the late 2000s, it initially declined from around 2000 to 2006.

What consideration of regional values of GDP shares obscures is that, in the case of China, the size of its rapidly growing economy supports the claim of its growing regional and global significance. Measured under purchasing power parity (PPP) assumptions, China's economy was the second largest in the world behind that of the US by 2003 (Costin, 2008). By conventional measures, China had become the world's sixth largest economy by 2003, fourth largest by 2005 (Costin, 2008), and second largest by 2010 (Hout and Ghemawat, 2010).

Figure 7.2 provides a more detailed breakdown of shares in world GDP sourced within the East Asian-Pacific region. What the relative stability of the East Asian-Pacific share of world GDP hides is a substantial shift in relative economic position of a number of major economies and groups of economies within the region. There has been considerable growth in the share of global GDP produced by China, consistent growth in the Association of Southeast Asian Nations (ASEAN) 10 group of economies' share of global GDP, and a significant decline in the share of world income provided by Japan, a set of features that have been followed relatively consistently

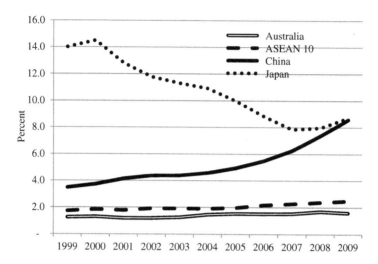

Fig. 7.2.   Shares of Global GDP within the East Asian-Pacific Region (% of World, Current US Dollars).

Source: World Bank, *World Development Indicators*, and author's calculations.

throughout the 2000s. Japan, in particular, has suffered a significant decline in terms of its share of world GDP, with this share falling from over 14% in 2000 to just under 8% by 2007. China, on the other hand, has enjoyed significant growth in its share of world GDP, reaching a point where the value of its output is essentially on par with Japan, from just under 4% in 2000 to over 8% by 2009, thus raising its economic (and potentially political) significance both within the region and globally.

Clearly, some of the above changes in the shares of global output in Figs. 7.1 and 7.2 can be explained through consideration of changes in the value of the US dollar against other major currencies, particularly the Euro, the Yen and the Renminbi (see Fig. 7.3). Indeed, some of the changes in the global share of GDP provided within Europe and Central Asia strongly reflect shifts in exchange rates relative to the US dollar (i.e., may largely reflect changes in the value of the Euro against the US dollar). This is particularly the case for the fall in share during the early 2000s, at which time the Euro weakened considerably against the US dollar (see Fig. 7.3). The increase in the Euro–US dollar rate by the end of 2009, to levels achieved around late 2007, would also explain some of the decline in the Europe and Central Asian share of global GDP observed during this latter period.

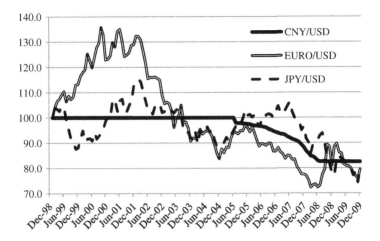

Fig. 7.3.   Changes in Major Currencies Against the US Dollar (June 1999 = 100).
Source: Reserve Bank of Australia, *Statistics*, and author's calculations.

While influenced somewhat by currency movements, Japan's share of global output has declined despite a general strengthening of the Yen against the US dollar since the early 2000s. However, the relative stability of the Chinese Renminbi–US dollar in the period 2000–2005 and that from mid-2008 (see Fig. 7.3), suggests that much of China's recent gain in global income share is due to its relatively rapid real growth in GDP rather than the influence of changes in the value of its currency. Thus real, rather than purely financial, factors appear to be generating the perceptions of the rapid growth in the economic significance of China.

7.3 Changes in the Global Financial Landscape

When considering financial development, a number of measures are, potentially, available. These include: bank deposits to GDP, stock market capitalization to GDP, and public bond market capitalization to GDP. However, consistent with the later discussion of large listed companies, the focus in this section will be on market capitalization.

With respect to major economic regions identified initially in Fig. 7.1, Fig. 7.4 highlights a significant decline in the global share of equity assets held in the North American region by market capitalization. However, unlike GDP, this has not been impacted as greatly by growth in the value and global

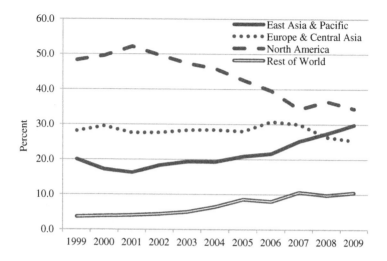

Fig. 7.4.   Market Capitalization of Listed Companies (% World, Current US Dollars).
Source: World Bank, *World Development Indicators*, and author's calculations.

share of European and Central Asian equity markets, which has been rela-
tively stable and even declined slightly over the period under consideration.
Most significant is the apparent rise in the share of market capitalization
held within the East Asian-Pacific region and in the rest of the world (Latin
America and the Caribbean, Middle East and North Africa, South Asia, and
Sub-Saharan Africa).

What is clear from the data presented in Fig. 7.4 is the impact of the
GFC from 2007–2009 on the North American share of global equity market
capitalization. Although recovering partly in 2008, the pattern of gradual
decline in the North American share of global market capitalization appears
to have been broken to some extent by the GFC. While a new pattern is yet
to emerge, the data from 2007–2009 suggests that the US share of global
market capitalization may have been stabilized, at least temporarily, rather
than declining more rapidly as a result of the GFC. This would be consistent
with the similarity in performance of the US equity market to that of Japan's
and the major European economies over the period 2007–2009 period (see
Fig. 7.6).

In following the country grouping of Fig. 7.2, Fig. 7.5 highlights that
within the Asian-Pacific region there have been greater changes in the
financial asset shares than those observed with the GDP. Japan's share of

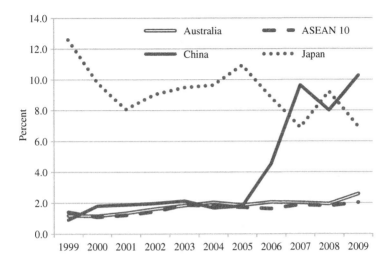

Fig. 7.5.   Market Capitalization of Listed Companies within the East Asian-Pacific Region (% of World, Current US Dollars).

Source: World Bank, *World Development Indicators*, and author's calculations.

global equity market capitalization has declined, although not consistently in level or rate, throughout the 2000s. More impressive than in the case of the GDP, has been the rise in China's share of global equity market capitalization, particularly commencing in 2005 (see Fig. 7.5). Also apparent in Fig. 7.5 is the gradual rise in the small but significant share of global market capitalization accounted for by the ASEAN 10 countries.

As with the shifts in the global shares of the GDP, it is necessary to consider the impact of exchange rate changes on regional and country shares of global equity market capitalization. In the case of the European and Central Asian regions, consideration of changes in the value of major global stock indices (see Fig. 7.6), suggests that shifts in index values are likely to dominate (e.g., as reflected in the Euro STOXX). This is also apparent in the case of Japan (TOPIX).

With respect to China, the relatively rapid increase in the value of the Renminbi to the US dollar during 2005–2007 must be credited with some of the contemporaneously observed gain in the US dollar value of China's global share of market capitalization. However, given the significant (although not consistent) increase in the value of its major market index since the late 1990s (Shanghai SE), and the relative stagnation of

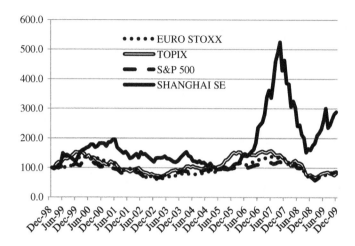

Fig. 7.6.   Changes in Major Share Price Indices (January 1999 = 100).
Source: Reserve Bank of Australia, *Statistics*, and author's calculations.

the major western markets, the increase in China's global share of equity valuation appears to be based largely on the relatively rapid growth of its equity markets. This relates to the significant financial deepening that has occurred in the Chinese equity markets as a result of the listing of former state-owned enterprises and strong growth in GDP.

7.4 Globalization, the Geographic Distribution of Control of Large Listed Companies, and the GFC

7.4.1 *Globalization and the rise of large multinational companies*

The recent shift of economic and financial powers towards China, especially within Asia (as per Figs. 7.2 and 7.5), is a trend that is expected to continue over the next two decades. While this expected shift in influence includes the continued movement of company headquarters to China (Hong Kong, Shanghai, etc.) (Albrecht, 2005), inward FDI to China may not be the major driving force. Given sizeable trade surpluses and a high savings rate, China is playing an increasingly important role as a source of finance within Asia (and globally) (Breslin, 2009). China's growing financial power is apparent in both its increased role as an international creditor, particularly of US dollar assets (Chin and Helleiner, 2008), and the growth in its role as a source of FDI (Zhang, 2009; Icksoo, 2009). It is also apparent from the growth in the relative global importance of its equity markets as highlighted in Fig. 7.5.

A link is often made between the process of globalization and the growth of large multinational corporations (de la Dehesa, 2006). China's rise has also been asserted to be the beginning of a "new phase" of globalization (Henderson, 2008). Thus, it would be expected that China's (and, more generally, East Asia's) growth in economic and financial powers would be associated with an increase in the proportion of large multinational companies' resident within its borders. For example, throughout its process of economic reform, China has focused on establishing a set of large, internationally competitive enterprises. This has recently included tying inwards FDI to its development policy [see Hout and Ghemawat (2010) on technology transfer]. However, China's success in achieving its objectives against a moving (and improving) set of leading firms has previously been questioned (Nolan, 2002), with few of the world's Top 1,250 firms residing in China and other high growth emerging markets (Nolan, 2010).

The interest in large, listed multinational companies reflects a variety of factors relating to their potential to exert political and economic power, and that this may be to the detriment of the developing world. In terms of economic and financial factors, the basis for this interest includes: the growth in the financial powers of multinational companies relative to governments (Farrell, 2008); that the shareholders of multinationals, and therefore the primary beneficiaries of profits generated, predominantly reside in high-income economies (Nolan, 2010); the dominance of multinationals in terms of control of FDI flows (de la Dehesa, 2006); and their dominance in the area of research and development, and thus technical progress (Nolan, 2010).

Although the data presented in Figs. 7.2 and 7.5 highlight the growing importance of China within the global economic and financial environments, based on the GDP and equity market capitalization, it is not apparent that China has to this point gained significantly in its share of control of these large multinational corporations. As noted, this focus on large corporations reflects their political and economic significance in determining both world trade and global capital flows. Thus, for China's position in the global economy to be cemented, we would expect to see a significant increase in its share of the world's largest companies.

7.4.2 *Globalization and the impact of the GFC*

The economic and financial processes of globalization are usually seen as occurring gradually. However, there are concerns that the GFC may have altered the pace at which each process evolves (Burrows and Harris, 2009). This includes the rate at which the progressive shift of economic and political power towards Asia, particularly China, is occurring (Overholt, 2010). To some extent, these concerns reflect the perceptions of the GFC as largely a North Atlantic phenomenon. Thus, the GFC is viewed as weakening both the US and Europe (particularly the United Kingdom) as global financial centers (Nesvetailova and Palan, 2008). That this event may add to China's perceived gains from globalization is also reflected in the tensions created by the large trade imbalances between the US and China (Bowles and Wang, 2008).

Against the view that the GFC is mainly a North Atlantic phenomenon, is acknowledgement of the widespread impact of the GFC outside Western Europe and North America (Wade, 2009). This includes the significant economic impact on China of the GFC (Wang, 2009), with China's real economy being particularly sensitive to global economic downturns due to its heavy reliance on exports (Palley, 2006; Breslin, 2009). Additionally, as a major creditor, China has faced significant financial costs throughout the GFC through the need to sterilize the impact of US dollar accumulation and capital losses on these US dollar holdings (Chin and Helleiner, 2008). However, as already noted, China has still been able to make significant economic and financial progress throughout the period associated with the GFC (Figs. 7.2 and 7.5).

7.4.3 *The geographical distribution of large listed companies and the GFC*

As argued above, the growth in China's (and East Asia's) economic and financial significance may be expected to be reflected in the proportion of large listed companies resident in the East Asian-Pacific region and, specifically, China (this would especially be the case given the size of many of the initial public offerings associated with the listing of large former state-owned enterprises). In Tables 7.1 and 7.2, large companies are proxied by the global Top 500 listed companies (based on the US dollar value of

Table 7.1. Region/Country Distribution of Top 500 Listed Companies.*

Region/Country	2006	2007	2008	2009
East Asia and Pacific	139	137	144	147
Australia	10	10	11	9
ASEAN 10	8	7	9	9
China	16	18	20	23
Japan	73	73	74	73
Europe and Central Asia	190	202	194	191
Euro area	122	130	124	115
Latin America and Caribbean	9	10	11	12
Middle East and North Africa	7	9	14	13
North America	141	129	125	121
United States	124	112	109	105
South Asia	6	7	7	10
Sub-Saharan Africa	8	6	5	6
Total	**500**	**500**	**500**	**500**

Source: *OSIRIS* and author's calculations.
Note: *Based on US dollar value of assets.

Table 7.2. Region/Country Distribution of Top 500 Listed Companies* (% of Total).

Region/Country	2006	2007	2008	2009
East Asia and Pacific	27.8	27.4	28.8	29.4
Australia	2.0	2.0	2.2	1.8
ASEAN 10	1.6	1.4	1.8	1.8
China	3.2	3.6	4.0	4.6
Japan	14.6	14.6	14.8	14.6
Europe and Central Asia	38.0	40.4	38.8	38.2
Euro area	24.4	26.0	24.8	23.0
Latin America and Caribbean	1.8	2.0	2.2	2.4
Middle East and North Africa	1.4	1.8	2.8	2.6
North America	28.2	25.8	25.0	24.2
United States	24.8	22.4	21.8	21.0
South Asia	1.2	1.4	1.4	2.0
Sub-Saharan Africa	1.6	1.2	1.0	1.2
Total	**100.0**	**100.0**	**100.0**	**100.0**

Source: *OSIRIS* and author's calculations.
Note: *Based on US dollar value of assets.

assets). While there has been growth in the number and share of these large companies domiciled in China (and to some extent East Asia) since 2007, the share of Chinese control of these large companies is still well below its shares of world GDP and equity market capitalization. Additionally, although China has made greater gains than other regions/countries in its share over the period associated with the GFC, these gains are still broadly comparable to those made by the Latin America and Caribbean and the Middle East and North African regions.

The advent of the GFC and associated corporate failures saw a significant decline in the number of US-based companies in the global Top 500 (from 124 in 2006 to 112 in 2007). However, since 2007 the rate of decline has been relatively slow (falling to 109 in 2008 and 105 in 2009). This may reflect, among other factors, the diversification of the US in terms of industrial structure (see Table 7.3). In particular, the US was not as overweight on financial-sector companies (banks, diversified financials and insurance)

Table 7.3.   Industry Composition of Global Top 500 and the US in Top 500* Listed Companies (% of Total).

Industry	Top 500	US	Top 500	US	Top 500	US	Top 500	US
Energy	4.4	6.5	4.4	6.3	4.8	7.3	5.0	5.7
Materials	4.4	2.4	4.4	2.7	3.8	1.8	3.8	1.0
Capital Goods	7.6	7.3	6.6	6.3	6.8	6.4	7.2	6.7
Consumer Discretionary	5.6	8.9	5.4	8.9	5.2	8.3	4.8	7.6
Consumer Staples	2.6	3.2	3.8	5.4	3.4	4.6	3.0	4.8
Health Care	3.0	8.1	2.8	7.1	2.6	6.4	2.6	6.7
Banks	36.8	15.3	37.6	16.1	39.8	15.6	40.4	16.2
Diversified Financials	8.8	16.1	9.4	17.9	9.0	18.3	8.6	18.1
Insurance	13.4	14.5	13.2	15.2	12.0	14.7	12.2	15.2
Real Estate	1.4	1.6	1.0	0.9	1.2	0.9	0.8	1.0
Information Technology	2.8	4.8	2.8	4.5	2.6	5.5	2.6	6.7
Telecommunication Services	3.0	2.4	3.2	2.7	3.2	2.8	3.4	2.9
Utilities	6.2	8.9	5.4	6.3	5.6	7.3	5.6	7.6
Total	**100.0**	**100.0**	**100.0**	**100.0**	**100.0**	**100.0**	**100.0**	**100.0**

Source: *OSIRIS* and author's calculations.
Note: *Based on US dollar value of assets.

as was the global Top 500 at the start of the GFC (see Table 7.3). At the same time, the US was relatively overweight in consumer staples, health care, information technology, and utilities, which may be less effected by economic downturns. Indeed, we can observe that as a percentage most of the fall in the US share of the global Top 500 occurred at the start of the GFC in 2007. Thus, this decline preceeded the fall in the shares of these large, listed companies in, for example, the Euro area, by one year. This reflects the earlier emergence in the US of the credit crisis, and the early collapse of a number of US controlled companies in the financial and consumer durables industries.

With respect to measures of the value of the Top 500 listed companies controlled within specific regions/countries, it is apparent that, following an initially large jump at the start of the GFC in 2007, the rate of decline of assets under North American (including the US) control has progressed at a relatively slow and steady pace (see Table 7.4). This decline has been exceeded in absolute level by the gain in China's (and the East Asian-Pacific's) share of Top 500 assets, some of which has been gained at the expense of the European and Central Asian and Sub-Saharan African regions.

Table 7.4. Region/Country Distribution of Top 500 Listed Companies* (% of Total Assets of Top 500**).

Region/Country	2006	2007	2008	2009
East Asia and Pacific	19.9	20.3	21.7	24.9
Australia	1.6	1.9	2.0	2.2
ASEAN 10	0.6	0.6	0.7	0.7
China	3.9	4.3	5.3	7.6
Japan	11.1	11.1	11.2	11.7
Europe and Central Asia	50.3	52.7	52.2	48.4
Euro area	32.0	32.8	31.6	29.4
Latin America and Caribbean	0.8	1.1	1.4	1.9
Middle East and North Africa	0.4	0.5	0.7	0.7
North America	26.7	24.4	23.1	22.8
United States	23.4	21.0	20.1	19.8
South Asia	0.5	0.6	0.5	0.8
Sub-Saharan Africa	1.4	0.5	0.4	0.5
Total	**100.0**	**100.0**	**100.0**	**100.0**

Source: *OSIRIS* and author's calculations.
Note: *Based on US dollar value of assets; **current US dollar values.

Table 7.5.   Region/Country Distribution of Top 500 Listed Companies* (% of Total Market Capitalization of Top 500**).

Region/Country	2006	2007	2008	2009
East Asia and Pacific	16.3	16.6	17.9	19.7
Australia	1.6	2.0	2.8	2.5
ASEAN 10	0.4	0.4	0.5	0.6
China	1.5	3.2	3.0	4.1
Japan	9.4	7.2	7.8	8.5
Europe and Central Asia	40.6	43.2	38.3	40.3
Euro area	21.6	24.5	21.5	20.8
Latin America and Caribbean	0.8	1.5	1.2	2.2
Middle East and North Africa	0.6	1.0	1.2	1.2
North America	41.1	36.7	40.5	35.2
United States	38.8	34.0	38.2	32.7
South Asia	0.2	0.7	0.6	1.1
Sub-Saharan Africa	0.3	0.3	0.3	0.4
Total	**100.0**	**100.0**	**100.0**	**100.0**

Source: *OSIRIS* and author's calculations.
Note: *Based on US dollar value of assets; **current US dollar values.

Given the volatility of stock markets globally during this period, the decline in the North American/US shares in the market capitalization of equity of these companies has been less consistent than that of assets (see Tables 7.4 and 7.5), although the pattern of change in this area reflects that in the US equity market overall (see Figs. 7.4 and 7.6). This observed pattern may also reflect measurement problems caused by fluctuations in the value of the US dollar against other major currencies, as discussed briefly above (see Fig. 7.3).

While hosting relatively few of the global Top 500 listed companies (see Table 7.1), the share in the global value of assets held by Chinese companies in the Top 500 has increased at a level commensurate with China's growth in its share of the global GDP. This reflects the very large size (at least in accounting terms) of some of China's relatively recent listings of former state-owned enterprises (e.g., the four large national state-owned commercial banks), and the intent of its industrial policy with its focus on creating large, globally competitive companies. However, 13 of China's 23 companies in the Top 500 in 2009 were banks, two were insurance companies, three were in capital goods, two were in telecommunication services, and three were in energy. Thus, China still lacks the industrial diversification attained by the US, potentially concentrating its global influence to a more limited range of industries than suggested in its growth in economic power.

7.5 Conclusion

As suggested at the start of this chapter, the intent has been to provide an overview of selected economic and financial changes that have occurred over the period associated with the GFC, and to address a few key issues. The first was whether the GFC has accelerated the shift of economic and financial powers towards the Asian-Pacific region, especially to China, and at the expense of the US as has been suggested in some of the political economy literature analyzing the GFC and its impact. The second was the impact of the GFC on the share of large multinational companies domiciled in China, an issue that has received limited attention. To this end, simple data on the relative position of countries and regions has been presented capturing GDP, market capitalization, and the value of assets, all measured at current US dollar values. It is this latter feature that must be recognized as a significant limitation of this overview, and one to be addressed in a more thorough analysis of these issues in the future. It is hoped that the conclusions reached here will raise sufficient interest, and controversy, to attract such additional research.

On the first issue, of whether the GFC has accelerated the shift of economic and financial powers towards the Asian-Pacific/China, it is observed that much of the overall decline in the value of North American/US share of global output is part of a trend that has been present over the 2000s. During this period, the East Asian-Pacific share of world GDP can be seen to have been relatively stable (and even declined until 2006–2007). In the area of financial power, as approximated by the share of global equity market capitalization, the picture is clearer. The East Asian/Pacific region has grown significantly in terms of its importance over the 2000s. However, in each case, the data suggests that rather than accelerating the economic and financial shift from North America, the GFC may have acted to (at least temporarily) stabilize North America's relative position. This reflects that, rather than being a North Atlantic event, the GFC was a global event which impacted more heavily on many regions outside North America than within the region, especially with respect to the relative decline in value of equity in the major economies that occurred during 2008.

The above does not detract from China's economic emergence. This is part of a longer-term trend reflecting China's relatively rapid growth in GDP over the 2000s, even if it is not an event associated strongly with the GFC (although during the GFC China has maintained a strong economic performance). Indeed, it is China's strong growth, supported by consistent growth in the ASEAN 10 economies, which has maintained the Asian-Pacific region's share of global output. This is in the presence of a significant decline in the share of world income provided by Japan. Thus we can see a shift of economic and financial powers not, *per se*, to the Asian-Pacific region, but to China (and regionally and globally away from Japan).

In the area of market capitalization, it is clear that China has provided most of the growth in the East Asian-Pacific region's share (supported by less spectacular, but relatively strong growth in Australia and the ASEAN 10 economies). It is, however, not clear that the GFC has provided the greatest impetus for this growth, with China gaining little in its share of equity market capitalization over this period. This is despite significant outperformance of its stock markets relative to major markets in the western world. Rather, it should most likely be seen as a direct result of the emergence and growth in the Chinese market oriented economy and financial system.

On the second matter of the impact of the GFC on the global share of large multinational companies resident in China (and expected as part of the ongoing process of globalization), while it is apparent that China appears to have made significant gains in share of the global Top 500 companies, it is also clear that it still holds a relatively small share of the total. This is even following the GFC and the North Atlantic regions' problems. Additionally, China would be expected to have gained a greater share of the global Top 500 listed companies over the second half of the 2000s. This is as a direct result of its continued listing of large state-owned enterprises (particularly banks), and the relatively rapid growth in its economy (and relative outperformance of its stock markets). Also observed was the relative lack of industrial diversification in those of China's large list companies that were included in the Top 500 by the US dollar value of assets.

Finally, the data presented in this chapter suggests that while severe in impact, the US does not appear to have had its relative global position weakened by the GFC to the extent expected by some authors (with respect to the large companies still under US control). To some extent it appears that it has benefitted from the well-diversified industrial structure of those US-based companies that were included in the global Top 500 used in this chapter.

References

Albrecht, T (2005). Where is the 'economic centre' of the Asia Pacific region? *J. Asia Pac. Econ.*, 10, 359–379.

Bowles, P and B Wang (2008). The rocky road ahead: China, the U.S. and the future of the dollar. *Rev. Int. Polit. Econ.*, 15, 335–353.

Breslin, S (2009). Understanding China's regional rise: Interpretations, identities and implications. *Int. Aff.*, 85, 817–835.

Burrows, M and J Harris (2009). Revisiting the future: Geopolitical effects of the financial crisis. *Washington Q.*, 32, 27–38.

Chin, G and E Helleiner (2008). China as a creditor: A rising financial power? *J. Int. Aff.*, 62, 87–102.

Costin, H (2008). China, an economic superpower: "Out of many, one?" *J. Transnatl. Manag.*, 13, 95–111.

de la Dehesa, G (2006). *Winners and Losers in Globalization.* Malden, MA: Blackwell Publishing Ltd.

Farrell, D (2008). New thinking for a new financial order. *Harvard Bus. Rev.*, 86, 26–27.

Henderson, J. (2008). China and global development: Towards a global-Asian era? *Contemp. Polit.*, 14(4), 375–392.

Hout, T and P Ghemawat (2010). China vs. the world. *Harvard Bus. Rev.*, 88, 94–103.

Huang, Y (2003). *Selling China: Foreign Direct Investment during the Reform Era.* USA: Cambridge University Press.

Icksoo, K (2009). Inward and outward internationalization of Chinese firms. *SERI Q.*, 2, 22–30.

Imai, K (2000). The government and enterprises — A changing relationship by market competition. In *IDE Spot Survey: China's Non-Performing Loan*

Problem, M Watanabe (ed.), pp. 12–22. Japan: Institute of Developing Economies.

McIver, R (2009). China's national banking system: Commercialisation and financial stability. *Int. J. Econ. Policy Emerg. Econ.*, 2, 391–414.

Nesvetailova, A and R Palan (2008). A very North Atlantic credit crunch: Geopolitical implications of the global liquidity crisis. *J. Int. Aff.*, 62, 165–185.

Nolan, P (2002). China and the global business revolution. *Cambridge J. Econ.*, 26, 119–137.

Nolan, P (2010). China's globalization challenge. *Copenhagen J. Asian Stud.*, 28, 63–82.

Overholt, W (2010). China in the global financial crisis: Rising influence, rising challenges. *Washington Q.*, 33, 21–34.

Palley, T (2006). External contradictions of the Chinese development model: Export-led growth and the dangers of global economic contraction. *J. Contemp. China*, 15, 69–88.

Wade, R (2009). The global slump: Deeper causes and harder lessons. *Chall.*, 52, 5–24.

Wang, X (2009). Chinese firms' corporate strategies in the economic downturn. *SERI Q.*, July, 32–39.

Zhang, K (2009). Rise of Chinese multinational firms. *Chinese Econ.*, 42, 81–96.

Zhao, Z and K Zhang (2007). China's industrial competitiveness in the world. *Chinese Econ.*, 40, 6–23.

Appendix A: Data Sources

GDP and total market capitalization data for countries and regions are derived from the World Bank, *World Development Indicators* (http:// databank.worldbank.org/). These are based on current US dollar values.

Data on the value of assets, market capitalization, country of registration, and industry for the global Top 500 listed companies is derived from the Bureau van Dijk *OSIRIS* database. Industry classifications are based on an aggregation into 12 industry groups (Energy, Materials, Capital Goods, Consumer Discretionary, Consumer Staples, Health Care, Banks, Diversified Financials, Insurance, Real Estate, Information Technology, Telecommunication Services, and Utilities) based on data derived at the eight-digit level based on the global industry classification standard (GICS).

For consistency with the GDP and market capitalization data, the global Top 500 listed companies are identified based on the current US dollar value of assets in each year.

Data on the level of major exchange rates is sourced from the Reserve Bank of Australia, *Statistics* (http://www.rba.gov.au/) database.

Data on the level of major stock price indices is derived from *Datastream*.

Part III
Macroeconomic Policy

Chapter 8

Intervention and Exchange Rate Regime Choice in Asia: Does the US Dollar Still Matter?

Tony Cavoli and Ramkishen S. Rajan

8.1 Introduction[1]

An enduring question in the literature on exchange rate regimes is: how do official classifications compare with *de facto* regimes? This chapter facilitates this comparison by presenting an analysis of the degree of *de facto* exchange rate flexibility in the exchange rate regimes for emerging Asian economies, viz. Bangladesh, China, India, Indonesia, Korea, Malaysia, Pakistan, the Philippines, Singapore, Sri Lanka, Thailand and Vietnam over the decade 1999–2009. We do this by employing one of the available and well-known methods — the Frankel–Wei (Frankel and Wei, 1994, 2007) methodology and employing this method to analyze exchange rate regime choice in the first and second moments, as well as controlling for regime type and assessing the dynamics of regime choice by controlling for time variation. The basic objective of this chapter is to draw inferences about regime classification from the Frankel–Wei estimates and then evaluate these with official and International Monetary Fund (IMF) exchange rate regime classifications.

We find that while there is evidence that suggests that there is greater exchange rate flexibility in Asia, the US dollar is still significant. There remains a high degree of potential fixity to that currency. We find that these results tend to correlate quite closely with the official and IMF-based classification for exchange rate regimes and that there are some pleasing results

---

[1]Much of this chapter draws on earlier work based on Cavoli (2010) and Cavoli and Rajan (2010).

when one controls for regime type. We find that those countries classified as inflation targeting countries tend to exhibit less fixity to the US dollar that those categorized as conventional exchange rate peggers.

8.2 *De Jure* Exchange Rate Regimes in Asia and the IMF Classification

Until 1998, it was fairly easy to obtain *de jure* exchange rate classifications as this data was compiled from national sources by the IMF. Specifically, between 1975 and 1998 the IMF's *Annual Report on Exchange Arrangements and Exchange Restrictions* was based on self-reporting of national policies by various governments with revisions in 1977 and 1982. Since 1998 — and in response to criticisms that there can be significant divergences between *de facto* and *de jure* policies — the IMF's exchange rate classification methodology has shifted to compiling unofficial policies of countries as determined by IMF staff.[2] While the change in IMF's exchange rate coding is welcome for many reasons (including the fact that the new set of categories is more detailed than the older one), the IMF is no longer compiling the *de jure* regimes. The only way this can be done is by referring to the website of each central bank or other national sources individually and wading through relevant materials. The results of this detective work are summarized in Table 8.1.[3] As noted, the IMF has replaced its compilation of the *de jure* exchange rate regimes with the behavioral classification of exchange rates. The new IMF coding is based on various sources, including information from IMF staff, press reports, other relevant papers, as well as the behavior of bilateral nominal exchange rates and reserves.[4] The third column of Table 8.1 categorizes Asian exchange rates based on the new IMF classifications as of July 2006.

As is apparent from the comparison within Table 8.1, India and Singapore are categorized as managed floaters, broadly consistent with their official

---

[2]The data has since been applied retroactively to 1990.

[3]The descriptions in Table 8.1 are mostly direct quotes from the official sources and not paraphrased by the authors and draws on Cavoli and Rajan (2009, Chapter 1) based on information as of mid-2008.

[4]Also see Bubula and Ötker-Robe (2002) which appears to be the intellectual basis for the IMF *de facto* regimes.

Table 8.1. *De jure* Exchange Rate Regimes in Asia.

Country	Official Policy Pronouncements (direct quotes)	IMF Exchange Rate Classifications as of April 2008[2]
Bangladesh	The exchange rates of the taka for inter-bank and customer transactions are set by the dealer banks themselves, based on DM and supply interaction. The Bangladesh Bank is not present in the market on a day-to-day basis and undertakes purchase or sale transactions with the dealer banks only as needed to maintain orderly market conditions.	Other conventional fixed peg arrangement (against a single currency).
China	On July 21, 2005, China announced the adoption of a managed floating exchange rate regime based on market supply and DM and with reference to a basket of currencies.	Crawling Peg.
India	The exchange rate policy in recent years has been guided by the broad principles of careful monitoring and management of exchange rates with flexibility, without a fixed target or a pre-announced target or a band, coupled with the ability to intervene if and when necessary.	Managed floating with no predetermined path.
Indonesia	In July 2005, Bank Indonesia launched a new monetary policy framework known as the Inflation Targeting Framework ... However, Bank Indonesia is able to take some actions to keep the rupiah from undergoing excessive fluctuation.	Managed floating with no predetermined path.
Korea	Inflation targeting is an operating framework of monetary policy in which the central bank announces an explicit inflation target and achieves its target directly ... However, the Bank of Korea implements smoothing operations to deal with abrupt swings in the exchange rate caused by temporary imbalances between supply and DM and, or radical changes in market sentiment.	Independently floating.

(Continued)

Table 8.1.   (*Continued*)

Country	Official Policy Pronouncements (direct quotes)	IMF Exchange Rate Classifications as of April 2008[2]
Malaysia	On July 21, 2005, Malaysia shifted from a fixed exchange rate regime of US$1 = RM3.80 to a managed float against a basket of currencies.	Managed floating with no predetermined path.
Pakistan[1]	State Bank of Pakistan has attempted to maintain real effective exchange rate at a level that keeps the competitiveness of Pakistani exports intact. [and] . . . does intervene from time to time to keep stability in the market and smooth excessive fluctuations.	Managed floating with no predetermined path.
Philippines	The adoption of inflation targeting framework for monetary policy in January 2002. . . . The Monetary Board . . . determines the rates at which the Bangko Sentral buys and sells spot exchange, and establishes deviation limits from the effective exchange rate or rates as it deems proper.	Independently floating.
Singapore	Since 1981, monetary policy in Singapore has been centered on the management of the exchange rate. (1) The Singapore dollar is managed against a basket of currencies of its major trading partners and competitors. (2) The Monetary Authority of Singapore operates a managed float regime for the Singapore dollar. The trade-weighted exchange rate is allowed to fluctuate within an undisclosed policy band, rather than kept to a fixed value.	Managed floating with no predetermined path.
Sri Lanka	The Central Bank continues to conduct its monetary policy under an independently floating exchange rate regime . . .	Other conventional fixed peg arrangements (against a single currency).
Thailand	Since July 2, 1997, Thailand has adopted the managed-float exchange rate regime . . . The Bank of Thailand will	Managed floating with no predetermined path.

(*Continued*)

Table 8.1.   (*Continued*)

Country	Official Policy Pronouncements (direct quotes)	IMF Exchange Rate Classifications as of April 2008[2]
	intervene in the market only when necessary, in order to prevent excessive volatilities and achieve economic policy targets. Under the inflation targeting framework, the Bank of Thailand implements its monetary policy by influencing short-term money market rates.	
Vietnam	Vietnam has adopted a crawling peg with the US dollar for its exchange rate.	Other conventional fixed peg arrangements (against a single currency).

Source: [1]Based on speech by former Pakistan central bank Governor (Husain, 2005). Compiled by author with assistance of Nicola Virgill from websites from various central banks and other official sources with minor modifications. Central Bank websites available at http://www.bis.org/cbanks.htm.
[2]IMF data on *Classification of Exchange Rate Arrangements and Monetary Frameworks*. Available at http://www.imf.org/external/np/mfd/er/2008/eng/0408.htm.

pronouncements. Vietnam, which used to be in this category, has more recently been classified as having a conventional fixed peg regime, in contrast to its official pronouncement of maintaining a crawling peg and band around the US dollar. Bangladesh and Sri Lanka have been characterized as fixers, despite their official declarations of being independent floaters. Pakistan is defined as a managed floater despite proclaiming to be an independent floater. Korea and the Philippines are characterized as independent floaters, consistent with their official assertions that they are inflation targeters. Indonesia and Thailand, officially inflation targeters, are classified as managed floaters. Contrary to the public pronouncement of the Chinese authorities that the currency is based on a crawling peg, recent empirical studies suggest the *de facto* regime appears to be a soft peg to the US dollar with the IMF classifying China under "other conventional fixed peg arrangements".[5] The Malaysian ringgit, since its official de-pegging, is defined as being a managed floater with no predetermined path. This is consistent with empirical analysis which suggests that the ringgit closely tracks a trade.

8.3 *De Facto* Exchange Rate Regimes The Frankel–Wei Method[6]

This section presents an analysis of the degree of *de facto* exchange rate flexibility in the exchange rate regimes for eight developing and emerging Asian economies that the IMF states are managed floaters, viz. Bangladesh, India, Indonesia, Malaysia, Pakistan, Singapore, Sri Lanka and Thailand. We also include the supposed independent floaters of Korea and the Philippines, since both countries' central banks have clearly also been intervening in the foreign exchange markets and built up reserves.[7]

8.3.1 *Model*

We present a model that has been recently used in Frankel and Wei (2007) as a way of incorporating exchange rate regime flexibility (or fixity) into the original Frankel–Wei (Frankel and Wei, 1994) method for inferring implicit basket weights involving the major G3 currencies.

Consider the following:

$$Intervention\_Index = \Delta e + \Delta r, \qquad (1)[8]$$

where, in order to facilitate the estimation of exchange rate regimes using Frankel–Wei, Δe, is defined as the local currency per some independent

[5]See Shah *et al.* (2006) and Ogawa and Sakane (2006) for empirical validation. Also see Eichengreen (2006) who provides a broader discussion of issues surrounding the Chinese currency and its exchange rate regime.
[6]This section draws on and updates Cavoli and Rajan (2009).
[7]We exclude the low income managed floaters in Southeast Asia, viz. Cambodia, Myanmar and Lao PDR due to data limitations.
[8]This is the same index used by Frankel and Wei. However, they use the term "EMP index" as opposed to "intervention index". The use of the first term can be confusing as the index used is not the conventional exchange market pressure (EMP) index commonly used in the literature.

numeraire — here we use the SDR[9] and Δr is the monthly change in net foreign assets (IFS line 11–line 16c) scaled by lagged money base (line 14).[10]

To see how it relates to the choice of exchange rate regime, we need to use an *Intervention_Index* to augment the Frankel–Wei method as follows:

$$\Delta e_t = \alpha_0 + \alpha_1 \Delta US_t + \alpha_2 \Delta JP_t + \alpha_3 \Delta EU_t$$
$$+ \gamma\ Intervention\_Index + \mu_t. \qquad (2)$$

The α coefficients in Eq. (2) are often interpreted as implicit currency weights. The G3 currencies of US dollar, euro and the yen (all per the SDR) are chosen as they represent world currencies deemed to exert sufficient influence on the local currency such that it is worthy of consideration in our estimates. While it is tempting to interpret these coefficients as potential basket weights, it is probably more prudent for them to be interpreted as "degrees of influence". The reason for this is that it is very difficult to say whether a high and significant coefficient value implies a basket currency, or merely market driven correlations.[11] Under Eq. (3.2), as $\gamma \to 1$, the exchange rate per local currency becomes more flexible as index 1 converges to the dependent variable, Δe and the α coefficients should be close to zero and/or statistically insignificant. As $\gamma \to 0$, the exchange rate becomes more fixed as the situation where reserve movements overshadow exchange rate movements is reflective of a sustained exchange rate intervention, and the extent of fixity to various major currencies is captured by the α coefficients.[12]

---

[9]The idea behind using the SDR revolves around finding a currency that is not excessively related to any of the currencies used in this study. A common choice in this literature has often been the Swiss franc, but there are concerns that its strong correlation with the euro may bias parameter estimates.

[10]Reserve differences are scaled by lagged domestic monetary base in order to compare the magnitude of the reserve change in relation to the stock of money base in the system. The result is an index that is more easily interpretable than if absolute values are taken.

[11]It is also for this reason that we did not impose the restriction that all the currency weights should add up to one or for that matter why we do not just restrict the parameters to take values in between zero and one (as there may be more complex correlations that we might know about *a priori*).

[12]In our estimations, we do not impose any constraints on the γ coefficient, thus it could exceed one or be negative.

8.3.2 *Static estimates by country: ordinary least squares (OLS)*

We use monthly data for the period 1999:m2 and 2009:m9, or sub-periods thereof depending on data availability. At this point it is worth advising readers to keep in mind that reserve values could change because of currency fluctuations.[13] Ideally, we should exclude these effects before estimation but are not able to do so since we lack data on the currency composition of reserves. This may impact the precision of the results in some cases. Table 8.2 presents the results. With the exceptions of Indonesia and Korea, the US dollar remains the currency that has the greatest degree of influence on the local currency. With the exceptions of Korea, Malaysia, Pakistan and Vietnam, the intervention index is highly statistically significant and therefore open to interpretation. The values are all under 0.1 in the cases of China, the Philippines, Singapore, Sri Lanka and Thailand, suggesting there exists a high deal of fixity in the local currencies (*vis-à-vis* a single currency or basket of major currencies). The intervention index has a slightly stronger economic weight in Indonesia, India and Taiwan, suggesting these two economies allowed relatively greater exchange rate flexibility than the others. The pertinent question here, as mentioned above, is to what extent are these weights market-driven versus policy targets?

We can attempt to answer this by summarizing the interaction between the currency weights and the intervention index. We focus first on those currencies with intervention indices that are at or close to zero and are statistically significant. The Chinese case is the most clear-cut with the US dollar weight at one, implying continued heavy exchange rate management.[14] The US dollar weights for the Bangladesh taka, Sri Lankan rupee and the Philippine peso are surprisingly large (0.9, 0.9 and 0.8, respectively), suggesting a high degree of fixity. While this is consistent with

---

[13]We prefer lower frequency data in terms of month-to-month changes as there is too much noise in low frequency data (day-to-day or month-to-month). High frequency data tends to tell us more about *ad hoc* interventions to minimize volatilities as opposed to degrees of influence of G3 currencies. In addition, the data on reserves are only available on a monthly basis so there is a practical dimension to our choice as well.

[14]The weight on the US dollar decline marginally if we consider the sub-period from 2006. The dynamic time path of US dollar peg is discussed later. The focus here is on point estimates.

Table 8.2. Frankel–Wei Estimates. Dependent Variable: Local Currency per SDR.

	Bang	China	Indon	India	Korea 1	Korea 2	Mal	Pak	Phil	Sing	Sri L	Taiwan	Thail	Viet
Const	0.10	−0.02	−0.51	−0.38	0.08	−0.30	−0.04	0.06	−0.05	−0.02	0.19	−0.32	−0.29	0.11
	(0.30)	(0.53)	(0.001)	(0.00)	(0.70)	(0.02)	(0.47)	(0.42)	(0.71)	(0.01)	(0.10)	(0.001)	(0.01)	(0.39)
Dollar	0.93	1.00	0.19	0.36	−0.23	0.40	0.77	0.98	0.80	0.32	0.94	0.45	0.38	0.78
	(0.00)	(0.00)	(0.31)	(0.002)	(0.38)	(0.01)	(0.00)	(0.00)	(0.00)	(0.00)	(0.00)	(0.00)	(0.00)	(0.001)
Yen	−0.001	−0.01	−0.20	−0.09	−0.19	0.32	−0.05	−0.02	0.004	0.04	−0.05	0.06	0.16	0.02
	(0.98)	(0.68)	(0.06)	(0.42)	(0.35)	(0.04)	(0.17)	(0.74)	(0.96)	(0.39)	(0.48)	(0.11)	(0.04)	(0.49)
Euro	0.08	−0.001	−0.03	−0.02	−0.33	−0.15	0.08	0.07	0.08	0.09	0.06	0.04	0.07	−0.04
	(0.40)	(0.97)	(0.87)	(0.83)	(0.03)	(0.25)	(0.26)	(0.54)	(0.41)	(0.10)	(0.56)	(0.48)	(0.43)	(0.68)
Int. Index	0.11	−0.05	0.36	0.25	0.001	0.02	0.01	0.01	0.07	0.03	0.05	0.10	0.07	0.05
	(0.08)	(0.03)	(0.00)	(0.00)	(0.92)	(0.09)	(0.24)	(0.75)	(0.004)	(0.00)	(0.05)	(0.00)	(0.00)	(0.40)
Adj R^2	0.70	0.96	0.77	0.63	0.13	0.28	0.65	0.64	0.39	0.30	0.62	0.52	0.36	0.67
DW	1.69	2.32	2.40	2.13	1.89	1.79	1.84	1.61	2.11	2.03	1.66	1.45	1.87	2.09
Sample	02m1: 09m3	01m3: 09m8	99m2: 09m9	99m2: 09m7	99m2: 09m6	99m2: 07m12	99m2: 09m4	01m3: 08:m6	99m2: 08m12	99m2: 09m8	01m3: 08m12	99m3: 09m9	99m2: 09m9	99m2: 09m2

Note: The table includes lagged dependant variables. Samples 1999m1 to 2008m9. Any deviation from this reflects the availability of data at the time of its acquisition. A one month lag dependent variable is included in all regressions and a one month lag term for the US dollar per SDR is included for China, India, Malaysia, Pakistan, the Philippines, Sri Lanka, Taiwan, Thailand and Vietnam if its inclusion helps to reduce serial correlation.

the IMF's categorization of Sri Lanka and Bangladesh as both having conventional fixed peg arrangements, it is at odds with the Philippines being described as operating an "independent floating" arrangement. Thailand and Singapore also have low and statistically significant intervention indices but with far lower US dollar weights and some positive and statistically significant weight to other currencies. This is indicative of management against a currency basket, consistent with the official proclamations by the Monetary Authority of Singapore as well as an often-noted desire for currency basket pegging by the Bank of Thailand. Both are broadly defined by the IMF as being managed floaters. Interestingly, if one truncates the sample to exclude the period incorporating the global financial crisis for the case of Korea, we find a pattern that is not dissimilar to that of Thailand, with strong influences by both the dollar and yen.[15]

Two other currencies characterized as managed floaters by the IMF are India and Indonesia. As noted, both have relatively higher intervention indices, suggestive *a priori* of a greater degree of exchange rate flexibility. The currency weights for Indonesia suggest it is market-driven as the α coefficients are either statistically insignificant (US dollar and euro) or zero (yen). The Indian rupee appears to have a degree of flexibility in the exchange rate with a possible loose US dollar peg. The intervention index measures for Korea, Malaysia and Pakistan are all statistically insignificant, implying there is insufficient evidence from the intervention index coefficient to suggest the existence of any systematic exchange rate fixity over the sample period under consideration. However, examining the α coefficients, one notes a high degree of influence of the US dollar and non-existent influence of the other currencies for Malaysia and Pakistan, suggesting that both countries manage their currencies against the US dollar.

8.3.3 *Estimates by regime type: fixed effects*

Thus far, we have generated estimates of the Frankel–Wei equation for individual countries. An interesting question that can be asked at this point

---

[15]This exercise was performed on all countries sampled. The results for Korea were found to be materially different for each sample period and are the reason why we noted this in the text.

relates to how clusters of "like" countries fare relative to each other. In other words, what is the US dollar coefficient, and the intervention index coefficient for countries that are "managed floaters" under the IMF classifications given in Table 8.1 versus those that have a conventional fixed regime or are independently floating? Furthermore, how do the coefficients compare for those countries that declare themselves as having an inflation target against those that do not?

Table 8.3 presents a fixed effects estimates for several panel data series' — each panel representing a regime type. The first and second columns of results present the estimates for the inflation targeters (Indonesia, Korea, the Philippines and Thailand) versus the remainder of the sample. The results show that the US dollar coefficient is lower and the intervention index coefficient is higher for the inflation targeting countries. This is broadly consistent with the normative literature on inflation targeting where

Table 8.3.   Frankel–Wei Estimates. Fixed Effects by Regime Type.

	Inflation Target	Not Inflation Target	IMF Indep Float	IMF Man Float	IMF Fixed
Constant	−0.12	−0.04	0.11	**−0.17**	**0.16**
	(0.32)	(0.28)	(0.48)	**(0.01)**	**(0.03)**
USD	**0.34**	**0.75**	0.27	**0.49**	**1.03**
	(0.01)	**(0.00)**	(0.11)	**(0.00)**	**(0.00)**
JPY	−0.06	0.02	−0.14	0.002	0.01
	(0.29)	(0.52)	(0.09)	(0.94)	(0.67)
EUR	0.18	−0.01	−0.09	**0.18**	0.08
	(0.08)	(0.85)	(0.51)	**(0.004)**	(0.18)
GBP	0.04	−0.05	−0.02	0.05	—
	(0.60)	(0.11)	(0.88)	(0.27)	
Intervention	**0.07**	**0.03**	−0.00	**0.09**	**0.04**
	(0.00)	**(0.00)**	(0.75)	**(0.00)**	**(0.02)**
R-sq	0.16	0.56	0.14	0.30	0.71
DW	2.09	1.95	2.01	2.00	1.89
X-sections/obs	4/408	8/706	2/198	6/604	3/185

Note: The table includes lagged dependant variable. Figures in parentheses are p-values and those parameters significant at 10% or better are in bold. Sample 1999m1 to 2008m9. Any deviation from this reflects the availability of data at the time of its acquisition.

a (more) flexible exchange rate is preferred under that regime. Moreover, the R-sq is lower. This is also reasonable to expect *a priori* as the nature of the estimates are such that they are deigned to uncover fixity.

The final three columns of results show the estimates for countries as grouped by the IMF *de facto* classifications — independently floating (Korea and the Philippines), managed floating (India, Indonesia, Malaysia, Pakistan, Singapore and Thailand) and conventional fixed (Bangladesh, Sri Lanka and Vietnam).[16] As with the inflation targeting results, the US dollar coefficient increases with the degree of (IMF *de facto*) fixity — although the floaters coefficient is significant only at 11%. The R-sq coefficient, similarly, is increasing. The intervention index is less emphatic since the value for the floating group is not statistically significant and near zero. The lack of significance for this group is possibly attributable to the fact that Korea and the Philippines and present quite different results individually. If we examine the managed floaters versus the fixers in isolation, we see that the index coefficient is lower for the fixers — consistent with the IMF regime classification.

8.3.4 *Dynamic estimates: recursive least squares (RLS)*

To further check if and whether there has been a change in the degree of intervention/flexibility in Asia over time, Figs. 8.1 to 8.4 present RLS estimates for the US dollar coefficient, α_1 and the intervention index, γ, respectively. The recursive estimates are generated by running the regression for Eq. (2) iteratively — beginning with k observations and recording the coefficient values until we reach the full sample as follows[17]:

$$\Delta e_t = \alpha_0 + \alpha_{1t}\Delta US_t + \alpha_2 \Delta JP_t + \alpha_3 \Delta EU_t$$

$$+ \gamma_t \ Intervention\_Index + \mu_t \quad \text{for } t = k, \dots, T, \qquad (3)$$

---

[16]China is omitted from this test as they are alone in being a crawling peg under the IMF classification.

[17]k is the number of regressors. Due to insufficient degrees of freedom, we discard the first few coefficient values — about three years' worth. Recursive OLS is a special case of the Kalman Filter modeling strategy with time-varying coefficients. These results are typically consistent with the rolling fixed window regressions where one would drop the oldest observation before incorporating the most recent.

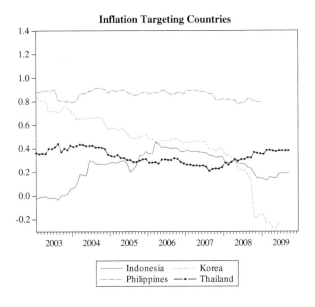

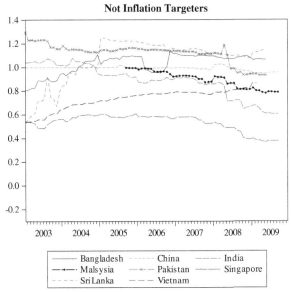

Fig. 8.1.   RLS Estimates for the US Dollar Weight.

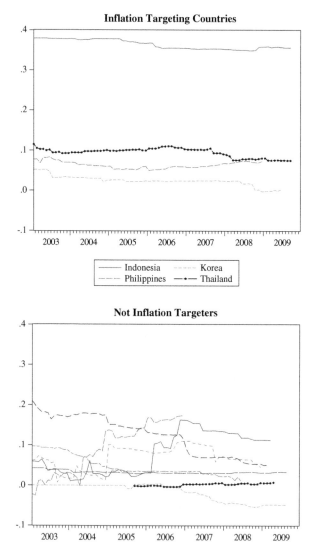

Fig. 8.2.   RLS Estimates for the EMP.

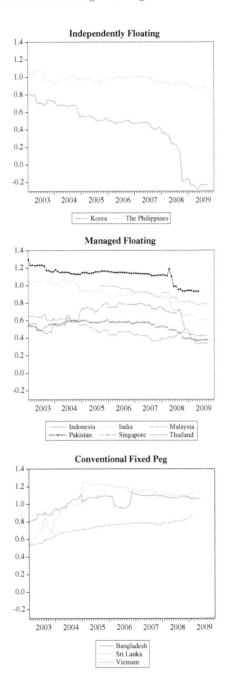

Fig. 8.3.   RLS Estimates for the US Dollar Weight.

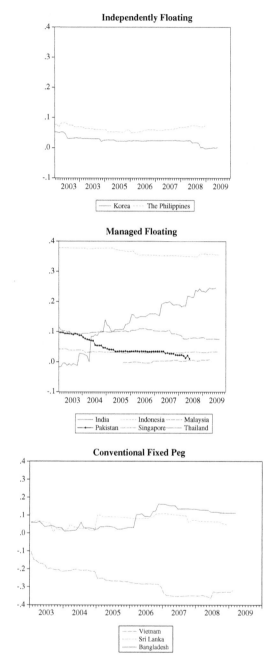

Fig. 8.4.   RLS Estimates for the EMP.

where, α_{1t} and γ_t, are the time-varying coefficients for the US dollar and the intervention index, respectively and T is the full sample under consideration for each equation. The estimates are derived by running the regressions as specified above (and as presented in Table 8.2) — but to avoid cluttering up the diagrams and highlight any possible influence of the recent global crisis, only the sample 2003–2009 is shown. The recursive estimates are grouped in precisely the same way as they are above in the section presenting the fixed effects model. This way, we can ascertain whether any patterns corresponding to regime type can be identified in the recursive series.

Figure 8.1 shows the recursive coefficients for the US dollar coefficient for the inflation targeting countries (Indonesia, Korea, the Philippines and Thailand) versus the remainder of the countries sampled — the non-inflation-targeters. We can see that, generally, the influence of the US dollar is lower for the inflation targeting group than in the other group. This suggests that the results show some conformity with the regime type. Figure 8.2 presents the recursive intervention index for the same pair of groupings. Indonesia stands out as a case where a higher degree of exchange rate flexibility is suggested. The others, irrespective of whether they are inflation targeters or not, appear to suggest reasonably high fixity (low coefficient values). One would have suspected *a priori* that the intervention index for the inflation targeters be systematically higher than for the others (Cavoli and Rajan, 2009).

Figures 8.3 and 8.4 present the recursive US dollar and intervention index respectively for groups of countries as they are categorized in the IMF classifications: independently floating (Korea and the Philippines), managed floating (India, Indonesia, Malaysia, Pakistan, Singapore, and Thailand) and conventional fixed peg (Bangladesh, Sri Lanka, and Vietnam). The picture is much less unambiguous here in that no clearly identifiable patterns emerge. The degree of influence of the US dollar is high across the board. From Fig. 8.3, while this is anticipated with the conventional fixed peggers, it is expected to be lower for the floating pair of Korea and (especially) the Philippines. The diagram for the managed floaters is, in some respects, consistent with that regime choice. The exchange rates in those countries with a lower US coefficient value — namely Singapore and Thailand — are also influenced by other currencies. The others tend to be influenced more exclusively by the US dollar.

A similar story emerges with the intervention series' in Fig. 8.4. With the exception of Indonesia with quite a high level of flexibility (as a managed floater), the degree of flexibility of all others are very low — even those countries classified as independent floaters.

8.3.5 *GARCH estimates*

In order to further inform the nature of intervention in the Frankel–Wei framework, we specify a basic GARCH model following the strand of literature characterized in Dominguez (1998) and surveyed in Guimarães and Karacadag (2004). The model is given as:

$$\Delta e_t = \alpha_0 + \alpha_1 \Delta US_t + \alpha_2 \Delta JP_t + \alpha_3 \Delta UK_t$$
$$+ \alpha_4 \Delta EU_t + \gamma \Delta f + \mu_t, \tag{4}$$

$$h_t = \lambda_0 + \tau_1(L)\mu_t^2 + \tau_2(L)h_{t-1} + \lambda_1 Abs(\Delta US_t) + \lambda_2 Abs(\Delta JP_t)$$
$$+ \lambda_3 Abs(\Delta EU) + \theta ABS(\Delta f) + \varepsilon_t. \tag{5}$$

The first equation is almost the same as that given by Eq. (2). The difference is that the *Intervention_index* term from Eq. (2) is now the change of net foreign assets scaled by money base, Δf. The reason for this pertains to Eq. (5) and will be explained below. For the most part, and despite the inclusion of GARCH terms, the α coefficients are similar to those given for the OLS model and are therefore not reported here.

As such, we will focus our attention on the conditional variance equation, Eq. (5) by presenting two sets of results; Table 8.4 presents the coefficients the exogenous variables to the variance equation, Eq. (5). Figure 8.5 presents the conditional standard deviations of the exchange rate series for each country.

The rationale for the analysis of the GARCH model is to assess how movements in the G3 currencies affect the conditional variance of the local currency. If $\lambda_1, \lambda_2, \lambda_3, > 0$, then this is suggestive of market driven activity in these currency pairs; volatility in one currency is transferred to another. If however, $\lambda_1, \lambda_2, \lambda_3, < 0$, this might possibly represent evidence of fixity in the 2nd moment — volatility in, say the US actually causes a reduction in the variation of the local currency. The same can be said for Δf. A negative θ suggests movements in reserves possibly designed to mitigate exchange rate volatility. The reason why the Frankel–Wei intervention term is not

Table 8.4.   GARCH Estimates.

	Bang	China	Indonesia	India^	Korea^	Malaysia
US dollar	0.06*	−0.05	−0.71	0.04	0.06	0.20**
YEN	−0.15	0.02	−0.01	−0.22**	0.84**	0.07*
EUR	−0.11	−0.01	0.63	0.06	−0.36**	−0.01
INT	−0.12	−0.13**	0.72**	−0.04	0.05	0.004
	Phil	Pakistan	Sing	Sri L	Thai	Vietnam
US dollar	−1.04**	−0.17**	0.06	0.03	0.16	0.08
YEN	0.04	0.04*	0.08	−0.20	0.68**	−0.15
EUR	0.33	0.09**	0.13*	−0.03	0.21*	−0.01
INT	−0.09**	0.05**	0.01	−0.01	0.08**	−0.11**

Note: *(**) refers to 5% (10%) significance and apply to z-scores in the variance equation. The intervention term, INT is not the index as described in Eq. (1) but the change in net foreign assets scaled by lagged reserve money (see main text for an explanation). ^Korea and India estimates are the period ending 2007m12.

used in this framework is that it cannot be interpreted in this fashion and, in fact, has no intuition under this model.

Table 8.4 examines the coefficients to each G3 currency and Δf. Results are mixed. There appears to be some possible policy-induced effects from the US dollar for Bangladesh, the Philippines and Pakistan, from the yen for Indonesia and from the euro for Korea, Pakistan and Singapore. The Δf term presents negative and significant values for China, the Philippines and Vietnam. Of those mentioned, the Philippines appears to be the most interesting. Recall that this is a supposed floater but presents quite significant evidence of fixity in both first and, now, in the second moment.

Figure 8.5 attempts to uncover the underlying flexibility of each local currency by presenting the conditional standard deviation. Again, results are mixed. It is clear that the floating countries of Korea and the Philippines appear to show greater flexibility than others, but perhaps not to the extent that might have been imagined *a priori*. There is considerable variation amongst the managed floating group, with Indonesia exhibiting much more flexibility than Malaysia, Pakistan and Singapore. Some of the conventional fixed peggers also exhibited quite high flexibility, more than some managed floaters. A possible reason for this is that some appear very focused on US dollar peggers; as such the flexibility may reflect cross rate variation that is not seen as important by authorities. A comparison of inflation targeters

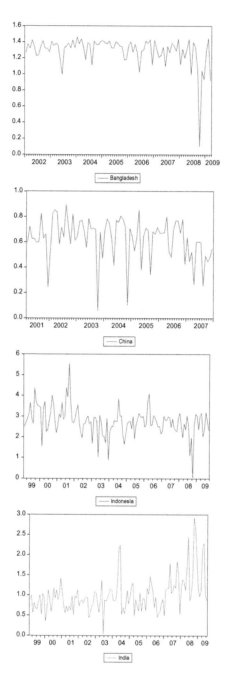

Fig. 8.5.   Conditional Standard Deviations.

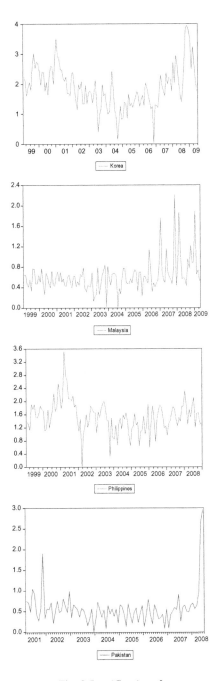

Fig. 8.5.   (*Continued*)

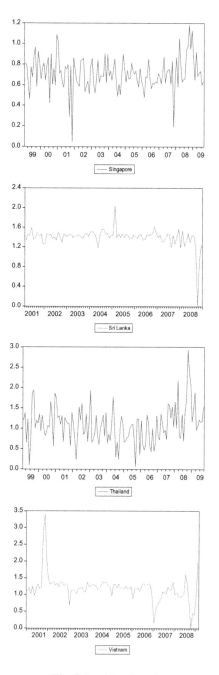

Fig. 8.5.   (*Continued*)

versus the remainder tends to suggest that they (the inflation targeters) exhibit generally higher flexibility.

8.4 Conclusions

This chapter has examined the *de facto* exchange rate regimes in Asia using the Frankel–Wei method and has presented results that examine the first and second moment characteristics of these regimes. We note that, as with most methodologies currently employed in the literature to measure *de facto* exchange rate regimes, the method used only captures a couple of the main characteristics of exchange rate regime choice. On the basis of the method presented here, there is a level of disconnect between the presentation of exchange rate regime and care must be taken to ensure that any regime classification captures all salient characteristics of the system in question.

There is some evidence indicating a greater degree of exchange rate flexibility in the regional economies — especially in South Asia. The answer to the question posed in the title of this chapter is "yes", there is still a high level of fixity to the US dollar — this occurs in almost all cases examined and occurs regardless of the *de jure* exchange rate regime.

While the propensity for foreign exchange intervention and exchange rate management among regional central banks remains fairly high in many cases and the degree of fixity to the US dollar remains very strong, we note that these relationships do correlate to some extent with both official classifications but less so with those based on the IMF exchange rate classifications. This is more likely to be the case when observing the degree of influence of the US dollar than in the intervention index. We find that the inflation targeting countries exhibit less fixity and are less influenced by the US dollar than the non-inflation targeters. We also find that the managed floaters (as defined by the IMF) exhibit less fixity and are less influence by the US dollar than the conventional peggers.

References

Bubula, A and I Ötker-Robe (2002). The evolution of exchange rate regimes since 1990: Evidence from de facto policies. Working Paper No. 02/155, International Monetary Fund.

Cavoli, T (2010). Exchange rate regimes in Asia: Intervention and the influence of the G3 currencies on Asian exchange rates. Paper presented at the Asia Pacific Economic Association Annual Conference, Hong Kong, 8–9 July.

Cavoli, T and RS Rajan (2009). *Exchange Rate Regimes and Macroeconomic Management in Asia*. Hong Kong: Hong Kong University Press.

Cavoli, T and RS Rajan (2010). A note on exchange rate regimes in Asia: Are they really what they claim to be? Mimeo, University of South Australia and George Mason University, June.

Dominguez, K (1998). Central bank intervention and exchange rate volatility. *J. Int. Money Finance*, 17, 161–190.

Eichengreen, B (2006). China's exchange rate regime: The long and short of it. Mimeo, University of California, Berkeley.

Frankel, J and SJ Wei (1994). Yen bloc or dollar bloc? Exchange rate in the East Asian economies. In *Macroeconomic Linkage: Savings, Exchange Rates, and Capital Flows*, T Ito and A Krueger (eds.), pp. 295–329. Chicago: University of Chicago Press.

Frankel, J and SJ Wei (2007). Estimation of de facto exchange rate regimes: Synthesis of the techniques for inferring flexibility and basket weights. IMF Annual Research Conference, International Monetary Fund, Washington DC, 16 November.

Guimarães, RF and C Karacadag (2004). The empirics of foreign exchange intervention in emerging market countries: The cases of Mexico and Turkey. IMF Working Paper WP.04/123.

Husain, I (2005). What works best for emerging market economies? Keynote address at the SBP Conference on Monetary-cum-Exchange Rate Regime, Karachi, 14 November.

Ogawa, E and M Sakane (2006). The chinese yuan after the Chinese exchange rate system reform. Working Paper No. 06-E-019, REITI, Tokyo.

Shah, A, A Zeileis and I Patnaik (2006). What is the new Chinese currency regime? Mimeo.

Chapter 9

Financial Instability Prevention[1]

Andrew Hughes-Hallett, Jan Libich and Petr Stehlik

9.1 Introduction

This chapter examines the extent to which a central bank or government should respond to the developments that can cause financial instability, such as housing or asset bubbles, overextended budgetary policies, or excessive public and household debt. To analyze this question we set up a minimalist reduced-form model in which monetary and fiscal policies interact, and where imbalances (asset or financial bubbles) can occur in the medium-run.

We then consider several policy scenarios with both benevolent and idiosyncratic policymakers. The analysis shows that the outcomes depend on a number of characteristics of the economy, as well as on the monetary and fiscal policy preferences adopted with respect to inflation and output stabilization. We show that for socially optimal outcomes, the prevention of financial instability should be carried out by: (i) both monetary and fiscal policies ("sharing region") under some circumstances; but (ii) by fiscal policy only ("specialization region") under others. There is however a moral hazard problem: both policymakers have an incentive to be insufficiently pro-active in safeguarding financial stability, and shift the responsibility to the other policy.

---

[1]This chapter uses results obtained from our earlier paper, Hughes-Hallett *et al.* (2011), and extends them to provide insights into the workings of the Asian economies as compared to the advanced economies of the Organisation for Economic Cooperation and Development (OECD). Details of the proofs of the various propositions used here will be found in that paper.

Under other circumstances, specifically where the policymakers act independently of each other, which is arguably the case in the advanced economies of the OECD (the US, Japan, Australia and most of Europe), we obtain quite different results. In this case where the policy institutions cannot cooperate with each other, we get all possibilities: financial instability is sometimes best countered by both monetary and fiscal policies together, sometimes by fiscal discipline only ("fiscal specialization"), sometimes by monetary policy alone ("monetary specialization"), and sometimes neither policy is able to mitigate the threat of instability ("indifference region"). It is possible to determine which region will obtain in any particular case, as a fairly complicated function of the potencies of each policy and the underlying policy preferences. This is in contrast to the situation where policymakers can cooperate in the pursuit of social welfare, in which case the best choice of policy to counter financial instability is simply a function of the relative potency of each policy. Ultimately however, in this case as in the others, the possibility of financial instability is due to over-ambitious governments, or governments that allow over-ambitious growth and employment targets to be imposed upon them. Weak preferences for curbing inflation or the absence of conservative policies are therefore not, in themselves, the root of the problem.

A third regime is one where the government delegates the conduct of monetary policies to a dependent central bank, to be carried out according to priorities and targets chosen by the government. This, arguably, is the situation in many (if not most) of the Asian economies. We find the best choice of policy to counter financial instability is now either to use monetary policy alone (monetary specialization) or by benign neglect (that is to use neither policy; the indifference region). The contribution of this chapter is to draw out these contrasts between Asia and the OECD economies.

These results can be related to the build-up of the current global financial crisis, and they have strong implications for the optimal design of the delegation process. The truth of the matter is that none of these policies were actually used, which may have been a contributing factor to why the crisis was so severe. Since the discussion has all been in terms of monetary policy reactions and financial regulation, none of the policymakers have aimed at maximizing social welfare. Benign neglect in the leading OECD economies allowed fiscal imbalances to build up in circumstances where both theory and popular perception, that monetary policies are more potent than fiscal, suggest either shared policies or a policy specialization should have been used. Likewise, the concentration on fiscal policies, with accommodating monetary policies, in the Asian economies before the crisis was the wrong strategy as far as preventing financial or asset bubbles is concerned. However, the more cautious approach to fiscal policy that has emerged in the OECD area, and greater use of monetary controls in Asia, gives us hope that the policy lessons may have been learned.

9.2 The Point of Departure

The policy question posed in this chapter is, to what extent should central banks or a government respond *ex-ante* to events that might cause financial instability: e.g., a housing or asset bubble, extreme fiscal policies, or excessive public or household debt?

The answer depends on certain characteristics of the economy, and also on the degree of ambition or conservatism in the policymakers. To be specific, we find circumstances where financial instability is best avoided by using: (i) both monetary and fiscal policies ("sharing"); (ii) and other cases when it is best to use only one of the policies ("specialization"); and (iii) still other cases where neither policy is needed ("indifference"). Moreover, there are circumstances under which one policy should be more active than the other, and also circumstances under which fiscal policy should care about nothing but the prevention of financial instability.

We also set out to determine how the policy-making process should be delegated when financial stability is likely and needs to be prevented. We find that neither a government nor its central bank should be allowed to select the degree of financial instability activism because of a moral hazard problem. Both policymakers have a strong incentive to be insufficiently pro-active and then shift the responsibility to the other policy. Our analysis therefore has strong implications for the way in which the policy-making process should best be delegated.

Our focus in this work is *ex-ante*, rather than *ex-post*. We concentrate on the best way to prevent financial instabilities or asset bubbles appearing. We therefore derive the optimal degree of financial instability activism using fiscal and monetary policies in order to avoid a possible crisis. We do not attempt to work out the best way to resolve and recover from any particular crisis after it has appeared.

Whether policymakers should in fact respond to asset prices has been examined many times in the past, and the consensus view has been clear. Movements in asset prices should *not* be included in the monetary policy rules since, if inflation is predicted correctly, the welfare benefits of doing so are minimal and the side effects could be damaging. This consensus view is perhaps best captured by the following quote:

> Once the predictive content of asset prices for inflation has been accounted for, there should be no additional response of monetary policy to asset price fluctuations. (Bernanke and Gertler, 2001).

There are many other papers that have argued along the same lines: see, for example, Goodhart (1995), Vickers (2000), Filardo (2000), Mishkin (2001), Gilchrist and Leahy (2002), Faia and Monacelli (2007).

But that consensus view proved to be increasingly controversial in recent years with a number of authors arguing that, under certain circumstances, having policies react to asset price changes, misalignments or bubbles can be helpful. For example, Cecchetti *et al.* (2002) demonstrated that central banks need to react differently to asset price misalignments than to changes driven by fundamentals. Since central banks can detect fundamentals, this could be done without having to impose specific target values for asset prices themselves. Likewise Bordo and Jeanne (2002) showed that asset price reversals can have a serious effect on real activity. But whether putting asset prices into the policy rule is helpful in stabilizing activity levels depends on the prevailing economic conditions in a rather complicated, nonlinear way.

In a more reflective piece, Bean (2003) argues that a credit crunch or large financial imbalances can and should cause a change in policy since price stability does not ensure financial stability or a low impact of financial balances/movements on activity levels. Bean therefore recommends a closer look at cases where credit expansion and asset price movements signal financial imbalances rather than a change in the fundamentals. That would imply discontinuities or possible regime switching, which is exactly what we discover below. This line of reasoning leads Wolf (2009) to argue that central banks must now target more than just inflation; which, in practice, is what the European Central Bank at least appears to do so (Siklos and Bohl, 2009).

9.3 Our Approach

We use a simple theoretical model (it is actually a reduced form of New Keynesian model), but for transparency and simplicity we prefer to use a minimalist reduced form rather than the structural models of previous studies in this area. If there is a role for financial activism, it is likely to be complex and nonlinear as noted in the references above (Bordo and Jeanne, 2002; Bean, 2003). Hence, transparency and analytic insights will be at a premium, for that a reduced form of the model is best suited.

We also use a general instability measure that can represent asset prices, house prices, public or private debt, a budget deficit, or a monetary or financial aggregate, etc. However, there are no additional policy instruments to achieve financial stability (e.g., capital cover, mortgage ratios, capital charges, Volker rules, transaction taxes, separate investment banking). Such regulatory instruments could be added later. Nevertheless, even then, under some circumstances (but not all), social welfare can still be improved using monetary and fiscal policies — by modifying the optimal reactions of each to the other. That shift could be interpreted as a measure of inter-policy coordination: policymakers are persuaded to move off their natural (in terms of their own underlying targets) optimal reaction functions to achieve better, or at least avoid worse outcomes through joint action.

9.3.1 *The policy set up*

There are two independent policymakers: fiscal (the government) denoted by F, and monetary (the central bank) denoted by M: their policy instruments are f and m respectively. Each policy has three objectives related to the stabilization of the level of inflation, π; the output gap, x; and asset growth gap, g; where the latter two gaps are the difference between the actual levels and some (correctly defined) natural levels. As discussed above, g will be interpreted broadly as the deviation of asset prices, property prices, public or private debt from some optimal levels.

Formally, the period utility of both policymakers, u_i, can be written as a function of their choice variables: $u_i(\pi; x; g)$. Woodford (2003) has shown that the first two elements can be derived from conventional micro-foundations. Further, we assume both policies can affect, at least under some circumstances, all the targeted variables

$$x(f; m); \quad g(f; m); \quad \pi(f; m). \tag{1}$$

These policy effects are then either direct (through the constraints of the economy), or indirect (influencing, via policy spillovers, the optimal choices of other policymakers). As Nordhaus (1994) shows, this set up implies policy inter-dependence: m becomes a function of f, and f is a function of m.

9.3.2 *Preferences*

The policymaker and society period utility functions contain three terms,

$$u_{it} = -\beta_i\left(x_t - x_i^T\right)^2 - \left(\pi_t - \pi_i^T\right)^2 - \lambda_i\left(g_t - g_i^T\right)^2, \tag{2}$$

where $i = \{F; M; S\}$ and S denotes the social planner (or society). The non-negative parameters π^T, x^T, g^T are the respective target values. Then, $\beta_i > 0$ and $\lambda_i \geq 0$ express the relative weights between the three stabilization objectives, where $\beta_i > 0$ is (the reciprocal of) the degree of conservatism. The $\lambda_i \geq 0$ weight expresses the degree of f-instability activism as well as the extent of f-instability aversion.

The fact that policymakers are averse to f-instability can be interpreted as an attempt to avoid potential imbalances in the future. Specifically, excessively volatile or rapid growth in some financial and real variables is likely to cause more volatile inflation and output further down the track, and is good reason for being concerned about the circumstances which could create such instability in the present.

In order to reduce the number of free parameters and the degree of heterogeneity, and to identify the main driving forces more clearly, we assume that the latter two targets are common across players and normalize them to zero

$$\pi_i^T = g_i^T = 0. \tag{3}$$

We now turn to the remaining target, x^T. We refer to it as the degree of ambition, and distinguish two types of players: (a) responsible with $x^T = 0$; and (b) ambitious with $x^T > 0$. To simplify the analysis here, we focus only on the scenario of most concern: where the central bank is responsible, but the government is ambitious [see, for example, Faust and Svensson (2002)]. We assume that society may be responsible or ambitious, but no more than the government in the latter case:

$$x_F^T \geq x_S^T \geq x_M^T = 0. \qquad (4)$$

The government's ambition either reflects that of society, $x_F^T = x_S^T > 0$, in which case the government is *benevolent*; or it is driven by other short-term political factors, $x_F^T > x_S^T \geq 0$, in which case the government is *idiosyncratic*. The main reason given in the literature for allowing $x_F^T > x_S^T$ has been the presence of certain political economy features, or to overcome the effects of distortionary taxation or monopolistic competition which prevent markets clearing at full employment. We exclude the case of $x_F^T < x_S^T$. This is because the society has a longer policy horizon, and hence discounts future ambition driven imbalances to a greater extent than does the government. However, allowing $x_S^T > 0$ recognizes that society may well not do that fully.

9.3.3 *The economy*

Our interest lies in being able to counteract financial instability in the medium term. To permit this, we will examine the performance and policy outcomes that obtain on average (over the business cycle) and are therefore unaffected by short-term zero mean shocks. Second, because of that, each policymaker will have perfect control over their instrument. Third, we will not include a long-term budget constraint on the government; but incorporate instead a less restrictive medium-run constraint in order to capture the excessive behavior observed in certain real world governments, and the consequences for financial stability.

We generate the dependence of outcomes on policy *via* the following Lucas-like supply curve relationship:

$$x_t = \mu\left(\pi_t - \pi_t^e\right) + \rho(G_t - \pi_t). \qquad (5)$$

This relationship can be derived from a New Keynesian model of the economy (Hughes-Hallett *et al.*, 2011). The π^e variable denotes inflation expectations for the coming period, which are formed rationally, in forward looking fashion, by private agents. Since the focus is on the medium-run outcomes, neither the details of the expectations process nor the shocks will affect our conclusions. The reader can however think of the standard $E_t\pi_{t+1}$ formulation.

The G variable is the instrument of F policy in nominal terms, and should be interpreted broadly as the medium-run stance of F policy. It can be thought of as all the F settings that will affect present or future revenues or expenditures. The current value could be summarized by the average budget deficit, or the growth rate of nominal debt as a percentage of gross domestic product (GDP). The future component may also include demographic factors that might affect future welfare, medicare and pension expenditures, as well as the expected value of any government guarantees made for private firms or banks. Growth in asset values, or the fiscal expansions or guarantees that underlie them, is the given by:

$$g_t = G_t - \pi_t. \tag{6}$$

The growth in asset values is therefore driven by excessive F policies, any guarantees extended to the private sector, public debt, low inflation, and hence, the low interest rates and excess private debt that may follow. Naturally consumption and investment would then expand, leading to an expansion in output as Eq. (5) shows.

9.3.4 *Policy framework*

As noted, we focus on steady-state outcomes only. M policy can then be represented by π_t. We refer to $\mu > 0$ and $\rho > 0$ as the *potencies* of M and F policy respectively.

9.3.5 *Institutional set up*

We examine both socially optimal levels of financial stability and those likely to obtain under existing policy arrangements. We assume that the central bank has instrument independence. Financial instability aversion parameters will be chosen during the game, but the degrees of conservatism are known before the policy game starts. We then consider three different institutional set ups:

(a) A social welfare scenario, W: where both λ_F and λ_M are chosen by S;
(b) A scenario with target independence for both players, I: with λ_M is chosen by M, but λ_F chosen by F; and

(c) A scenario with target dependence at the central bank, D; where both λ_F and λ_M are chosen by F.

In each case, after observing the λ choice, players set their policies independently; that is, they move simultaneously while retaining instrument independence in each case. The only exception is that there is only one player in the social welfare scenario. These policy choices then get repeated in each steady state.

9.3.6 Optimal policy choices

To derive macroeconomic outcomes in this set up, we need to solve backwards, treating the λ values as known. Using preferences, (2)–(4), and constraints, (5)–(6), we get the following reaction functions under rational expectations:

$$\pi_t = \frac{G_t[\rho\beta_M(\rho - \mu) + \lambda_M]}{1 + \rho\beta_M(\rho - \mu) + \lambda_M} \quad \text{and} \quad G_t = \frac{\pi_t(\lambda_F + \rho^2\beta_F) + \rho\beta_F x_F^T}{\lambda_F + \rho^2\beta_F}.$$

$$(7)$$

Solving these reaction functions together, we obtain the following policy choices:

$$g^* = \frac{x_F^T \beta_F \rho}{\beta_F \rho^2 + \lambda_F}, \quad \pi^* = [\rho\beta_M(\rho - \mu) + \lambda_M]g^* \qquad (8)$$

together with the general (fiscal) stance of the economy $G^* = g^* + \pi^*$ and $x^* = g^* \cdot \rho$.

Notice that, if $x_F^T = 0$, all variables are at their long-run optimal values and there will be no imbalances in the economy. We therefore need to consider only $x_F^T > 0$.

We can think of $g^* > 0$ as a bubble. From (8), it is evident that the size of the bubble is increasing in F's ambition x_F^T but decreasing in F's aversion to financial instability λ_F. This will naturally affect the socially optimal value of λ_F. Further, while M's aversion to financial instability, λ_M, does nothing to determine the size of the bubble, it does affect the incentives of the government to act, and hence the eventual stance of F policy.

9.4 Choosing Risk/Financial Instability Aversion

Now, we define regions of financial instability and financial policy aversion based on the values of λ_i^j, $j = \{scenarios\ W, I, D\}$ and $i = \{F, M\}$. We get the following:

(1) Sharing: both policies are active, $\min\{\lambda_M^j, \lambda_F^j\} > 0$.
(2) Specialization: one policy is passive and the other active or ultra-active:

    (a) *M*-specialization: *M* policy is the active one, $\lambda_M^j > \lambda_F^j = 0$,
    (b) *F*-specialization: *F* policy is the active one, $\lambda_F^j > \lambda_M^j = 0$.

(3) Indifference: both policies are passive, $\lambda_M^j = \lambda_F^j = 0$.

9.4.1 *Welfare scenario, W*

Substitute the equilibrium values given by (8) into $u_{S,t}$. Take derivatives with respect to both λ_M and λ_F, set equal to zero, and solve jointly. We get:

$$\lambda_M^W = \beta_M \rho (\mu - \rho) \quad \text{if } \rho < \mu, \text{ but } zero \text{ otherwise; and}$$
$$\lambda_F^W = \beta_F \left[x_F^T (\lambda_S + \beta_S \rho^2) / (x_S^T \beta_S) - \rho^2 \right] \text{ if } x_S^T > 0, \text{ but } zero \text{ if } x_S^T = 0.$$
$$(9)$$

This result, as it stands, does not make it clear which policy or policies should best be directed at preserving financial stability, or when, or how strongly. Nevertheless, we can infer the following:

Proposition 1. *In the welfare scenario: both policies should either be active (**sharing region**), or fiscal policy should be active and monetary passive (**F-specialization region**). The M-specialization (monetary policy active, fiscal passive) and indifference regions do not occur in this equilibrium. Both would ignore financial instability.*

In addition, whether we should follow the sharing or an *F*-specialization strategy depends on the following relative policy potencies.

Proposition 2 (comparative advantage). *If F policy is more potent, then it should be the only active policy (ultra active if $\lambda = \infty$). If F is less potent, both should be active; and if M policy is more potent by enough it should be the more active of the two: if $\mu > \rho + \lambda_F^W$.*

Finally, in view of (9), it is clear that there are sets of circumstances under which society will find it optimal to appoint M and F policymakers that are: (i) active even if society disregards financial instability altogether $\lambda_S = 0$; or (ii) passive even if society is averse to financial instability to any degree $\lambda_S > 0$.

Proposition 3. *In the welfare scenario, the degree of M financial instability aversion is weakly decreasing in (is weakly substituted by) central bank conservatism. By contrast, the degree of F financial instability aversion (policy activism) is weakly increasing in λ_S, x_F^T / x_S^T, ρ and β_F as one might expect; but decreasing in β_S; and, most significantly, independent of the preferences and targets for monetary policy.*

Hence, the more ambitious the society, the more it appoints less pro-active/less regulated F policymakers. Society's preferences hinder financial stability *via* economic ambition and by electing less pro-active governments.

9.4.2 *Independence scenario, I*

In this scenario each policymaker chooses independently, but simultaneously, their own λ value. To analyze this case, substitute the equilibrium outcomes from (8) into u_{Mt} and u_{Ft}; differentiate with respect to λ_F and λ_M respectively, and set equal to zero. Solving these two conditions jointly yields:

$$\lambda_F^I = 0.5 - \beta_F \rho^2 \text{ if } \rho < \bar{\rho}, \text{ but } zero \text{ otherwise; and}$$
$$\lambda_M^I = \rho(\mu - \rho)\beta_M - 0.5 \text{ if } \mu \geq \bar{\mu}, \text{ but } zero \text{ if } \mu < \bar{\mu}, \tag{10}$$

where $\bar{\mu} = \rho + (2\rho\beta_M)^{-1}$ and $\bar{\rho} = (2\beta_F)^{-1/2}$. This leads us to:

Proposition 4. *In the independence scenario, we now can find ourselves in any region: sharing, M-specialization, F-specialization, as well as indifference. However, no circumstances exist under which a policy is ultra-active.*

It turns out there are three risk/financial instability regions in this solution (see Fig. 9.1):

(1) Where λ_F is increasing in λ_M. High values of λ_M increase π^*. In those cases, the central bank is unable to stop the government increasing debt;

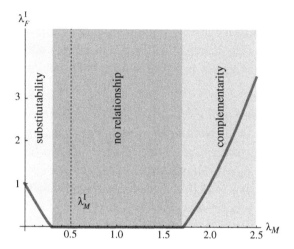

Fig. 9.1.   An Example of λ_F as a Function of λ_M for Values $\beta_F = \beta_M = 1$; $\rho = 1, \mu = 2$.

all it can do is let inflation rise to deflate it (a fiscal theory of the price level).

(2) Where λ_F is decreasing in λ_M. When the latter increases, there is less need for fiscal activism but that means less output expansion and a tendency to deflation.

(3) No relationship, no substitution or complementarity.

9.4.2.1 *Conclusion*

In the independence scenario, the M policymakers can indirectly induce F policy to be active and instability averse; that is, monetary policy can in certain circumstances discipline the fiscal policymakers.

9.4.3 *Dependence Scenario, D*

In this scenario, the government chooses its own value of λ_F while delegating λ_M to the central bank. Analogously to the welfare case, substitute the equilibrium outcomes from (8) into u_{Ft}; differentiate with respect to λ_M and λ_F; set equal to zero, and solve jointly to obtain

$$\lambda_M^D = \lambda_M^W \quad \text{and} \quad \lambda_F^D = 0. \tag{11}$$

The possible outcomes for the dependence scenario are therefore:

Proposition 5. *With dependence, we obtain either the indifference or M-specialization regions. There are no parameter values yielding F-specialization or sharing, or an ultra-active policy.*

Moral hazard issues: Note that neither policy's activism, in either the I or D scenarios, is a function of λ_S — unlike λ_F in the welfare scenario.

Proposition 6 (*F*'s moral hazard). *In the dependence scenario, the government will choose F activism to be less than or equal to the value that: (i) it delegates to the central bank $\lambda_F^D \leq \lambda_M^D$; and (ii) that it chooses for itself in the independence scenario $\lambda_F^D \leq \lambda_F^I$.*

This proposition demonstrates that the government has an incentive to "pass the buck", and leave it up to the central bank to deal with the consequences of its excessively ambitious fiscal policies. As λ_F affects F's utility both through the outcomes and through the impact which a given outcome has on the government, ambitious F policymakers may choose a low λ_F to avoid responsibility for these outcomes.

Proposition 7 (*M*'s moral hazard). *In the independence scenario, the central bank will choose a level of M activism less than or equal to: (i) the socially optimal value $\lambda_M^I \leq \lambda_M^W$; and (ii) the value delegated to the bank by the government in the dependence scenario $\lambda_M^I \leq \lambda_M^D$.*

As this analysis implies, the price to pay for preventing instability in the financial system is the need to deviate from the inflation target. The fact that central banks are accountable for achieving the target may be a good part of why inadequate effort was put into combating financial instability in so many countries.

Proposition 7 also implies that, in the independence scenario, a government's influence over the central bank is limited. Since an independent bank is inclined to be less active than it should, the government sometimes needs to step in to make up for it; that is, compensate for the sub-optimally low λ_M. Thus:

Proposition 8. *In the independence scenario, the government may choose its activism to be more than the value assigned to it in the welfare scenario*

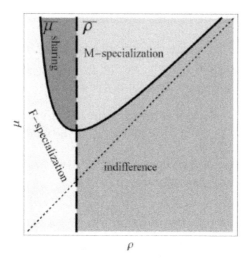

Fig. 9.2.   The Possible Regions in the Independence Scenario (with $\beta_F = \beta_M = 1$).

$\lambda_F^I > \lambda_F^I$. *The government is being forced to compensate for inadequate prudential activity by the central bank; that is to provide discipline by default.*

Proposition 9. *In the independence scenario, unlike in the welfare and dependence scenarios, M policy may end up being the more (or the only) active policy despite being less potent.*

This last result can be seen graphically in Fig. 9.2, and implies that the outcomes may contradict the principle of comparative advantage reported in Proposition 2. It provides further evidence of the shortcomings of the delegation process.

9.5 Conclusions

This chapter examines how strongly, if at all, monetary and fiscal policies should respond, pre-emptively, to phenomena that can cause financial imbalances, instability, or asset price bubbles. The answer turns out to depend on a number of factors related to the structure of the economy, and to the preferences of society or the policymakers.

However, the pattern of the results is rather complicated. There are circumstances in which the burden of preventing financial instability and bubbles should be borne by monetary policies, others when it should be the responsibility of fiscal policy, and still others when both policies are needed (with one or other in a leadership role). And there are still other situations when neither policy should be involved.

This leads to the rather startling conclusion that there will be cases where prudential policies should be put in place although the public has no interest in having policies that safeguard against possible financial instability; and also many cases where policies will provide no protection against instability despite the public clearly wanting protection. In addition, there will clearly be cases where the wrong policy has been allocated the lead role in preserving financial stability; and cases where public preferences lead to governments that ignore the financial stability issue, or adopt a regime of light regulation, although the situation clearly calls for prudential (instability averse) policies.

These results clearly resonate with what we have observed in the recent financial crisis. The examples from recent history are many: lax and over-ambitious policies when some (perhaps now with the benefit of hindsight) were calling for greater caution; or prudential policies when others were calling/lobbying for the constraints to be lifted or regulations lightened; cases where the responsibility for financial supervision and regulation has oscillated back and forth between government and the central bank or a third party on the argument that it was previously allocated to the wrong policy (agency); the lengthy academic debates on whether monetary or fiscal policies ought to be designed to react to financial imbalances and bubbles; governments and bankers who have consciously taken a "hands off" approach to financial imbalances as a matter of principle although there were clear concerns in the economy itself. Any of these cases could easily be explained, and resolved, through the results of our analysis.

Finally, we find that neither governments nor central banks should be allowed to choose their own degree of financial instability aversion because of a moral hazard problem. Both policymakers have an incentive not to allocate sufficient effort to supervision and prudential policies, and to shift the responsibility for such efforts to the other policymaker. The precise structure of the delegation process — that part which determines the incentives of the policymakers to be prudent — therefore plays an important role in preserving financial stability.

What do these results imply for the Asian versus OECD economies comparison?

(1) First, the socially optimal/first best outcomes can never be achieved in the dependence regime, whereas they can be achieved in the independence scenario under a range of parameter values. In those circumstances, the independence scenario will dominate the dependence regime.
(2) However, there is also a range of parameter values for which the ranking is reversed.

There is a threshold value for the public's aversion to financial stability, λ_S, such that when the public is unconcerned dependence delivers better results than independence. Conversely, independence is better when the public becomes concerned. The formula for that threshold value is rather complicated (Hughes-Hallett *et al.*, 2011, Eq. (21)). But, for plausible parameter values, it is increasing the larger is the public's ambition for growth (x_S^T), the higher is the priority for growth over controlling inflation (β_F), the more potent is fiscal policy (ρ). Consequently, to the extent it is correct to say that the Asian economies have typically chosen the dependence route, while the more inflation conscious OECD economies have chosen independence regimes, then the Asians may have chosen the better regime for their circumstances (ambitious growth, low public concern for financial stability, a higher inflation tolerance, higher impact fiscal policies) — although they will never achieve socially optimal outcomes. The OECD have probably also chosen the best regime for their circumstances, and could achieve the social optimum.

Hence, the real distinction is: the Asians have left themselves open and prone to financial instability, with a low public demand and consequently a low supply of macro-prudential policies to combat such instabilities. One imagines a rollercoaster ride, with bubbles and imbalances appearing and disappearing. The OECD economies have chosen a regime which allows macro-prudential policies to be deployed, and potentially to good (social) effect. But whether their policymakers will make use of this opportunity after the current crisis is resolved remains to be seen.

References

Bean, CR (2003). Asset prices, financial imbalances and monetary policy: Are inflation targets enough? In *Asset Prices and Monetary Policy*. Sydney: Reserve Bank of Australia.

Bernanke, B and ML Gertler (2001). Should central banks respond to movements in asset prices? *Am. Econ. Rev.*, 91(2), 253–257.

Bordo, M and O Jeanne (2002). Monetary policy and asset prices: Does benign neglect make sense? *Int. Finance*, 5(2), 139–164.

Cecchetti, S, H Genberg and S Wadhwani (2002). Asset prices in a flexible inflation targeting framework. In *Asset Price Bubbles: Implications for Monetary, Regulatory and International Policies*, W Hunter, G Kaufman and M Pomerleano (eds.). Cambridge: MIT Press.

Faia, E and T Monacelli (2007). Optimal interest rates, asset prices and credit frictions. *J. Econ. Dyn. Control*, 31(10), 3228–3254.

Faust, J and LEO Svensson (2002). The equilibrium degree of transparency and control in monetary policy. *J. Money Credit Banking*, 34(2), 520–539.

Filardo, AJ (2000). Monetary policy and asset prices. *Fed. Res. Bank Kansas City Econ. Rev.*, Q3, 11–37.

Gilchrist, S and J Leahy (2002). Monetary policy and asset prices. *J. Monetary Econ.*, 49(1), 75–97.

Goodhart, C (1995). Price stability and financial stability. In *The Central Bank and the Financial System*, C Goodhart (ed.). Cambridge: MIT Press.

Hughes-Hallett, A, J Libich and P Stehlík (2011). Macro-prudential policies and financial stability. *Econ. Record*, 87(277), 318–334.

Mishkin, FS (2001). The transition mechanism and the role of asset prices. NBER Working Paper No. 8617, Cambridge, MA.

Nordhaus, W (1994). Policy games: Coordination and independence in monetary and fiscal policies. *Brookings Pap. Eco. Ac.*, 25(2), 139–216.

Siklos, P and M Bohl (2009). Asset prices as indicators of euro area monetary policy: An empirical assessment of their role in a Taylor rule. *Open Econ. Rev.*, 20(1), 39–60.

Vickers, J (2000). Monetary policy and asset prices. *Manchester School*, 68(s1), 1–22.

Wolf, M (2009). Central banks must target more than just inflation. *Financial Times*, 6 May 2009.

Woodford, M (2003). *Interest and Prices*. Princeton, NJ: Princeton University Press.

Index